T0316831

British Society for International Understanding

BRITISH SURVEY HANDBOOKS

General Editor: JOHN EPPSTEIN

IV

HUNGARY

BRITISH SURVEY HANDBOOKS

HUNGARY

CAMBRIDGE

AT THE UNIVERSITY PRESS

1945

CAMBRIDGE
UNIVERSITY PRESS

University Printing House, Cambridge CB2 8BS, United Kingdom

Cambridge University Press is part of the University of Cambridge.

It furthers the University's mission by disseminating knowledge in the pursuit of education, learning and research at the highest international levels of excellence.

www.cambridge.org
Information on this title: www.cambridge.org/9781107426122

© Cambridge University Press 1945

This publication is in copyright. Subject to statutory exception and to the provisions of relevant collective licensing agreements, no reproduction of any part may take place without the written permission of Cambridge University Press.

First published 1945
First paperback edition 2014

A catalogue record for this publication is available from the British Library

ISBN 978-1-107-42612-2 Paperback

Additional resources for this publication at www.cambridge.org/9781107426122

Cambridge University Press has no responsibility for the persistence or accuracy of URLs for external or third-party internet websites referred to in this publication, and does not guarantee that any content on such websites is, or will remain, accurate or appropriate.

CONTENTS

CONTENTS

Folding Map

available for download from www.cambridge.org/9781107426122

EDITOR'S NOTE

The standard works on the history and economy of Hungary have been freely used in the compilation of this small book to complement my own vivid recollections, but inadequate knowledge of that country between the two wars, and the best available official and other sources of information have been employed to illuminate the events of the last five years.

Two of the first four Handbooks in this series have been devoted to Allied countries, Belgium and Greece, two to ex-enemy countries, Rumania and Hungary. The reader will observe that exactly the same method has been employed, and that the same spirit has informed the treatment of each of them. We are not concerned so much to distribute praise or blame as to describe realities and to explain historically the causes, whose effects are seen in the part which each country has been playing in the drama of contemporary Europe, and in the internal developments of the country. If in each case the writers or compilers have erred from cold impartiality in the direction of sympathy with the common people, they and I have erred deliberately. *Non intratur in veritatem nisi per caritatem.* It is not by a censorious approach or subservience to the slogans of war-time propaganda that the real forces at work in another nation can be understood, but by a serious effort to 'get inside the minds' of its people; it is a difficult task at the best of times, but one which it is more than worth while for those to attempt whose object is the truth.

EDITOR'S NOTE

The bulk of this Handbook was written before the war in Hungary had reached its climax. It has been brought up to date, at the time of going to press, by the inclusion of the Armistice Terms and the composition and programme of the Provisional Government of Debreczen. The final reduction of the German garrison in Budapest by the Red Army is assumed: no prophecy of subsequent developments of Russian policy in this part of Europe is essayed.

JOHN EPPSTEIN

January 1945

HUNGARY

CHAPTER I

THE OLD HUNGARY, A.D. 900–1919

THE IMPORTANCE OF THE PAST. The occupation of Hungary by the Red Army, the overthrow of the system imposed on the country by Germany and the substitution for it of new and radically different elements are already a matter of history. But the future of Hungary is still obscure, and the problem of the Hungarian nation, an integral part of the European scene for over a thousand years, will be with us so long as Europe lasts. It is, therefore, more than ever necessary to understand the mentality and characteristics of this people, the economic as well as political position of Hungary in the Danubian basin and the reasons which underlie the antagonisms which separate the Magyars from their neighbours surrounding the Hungarian plain. For these purposes it is necessary, more perhaps than in the case of any other European people, to study their evolution in history; for they are pre-eminently the children of their own past. Without a knowledge of that past, it is impossible to understand the stages of the tragedy which has brought Hungary to its present plight. It is not, however, the only or the main object of this small book to trace the political development of Hungary; like all the handbooks in the present series, and like the *British Society for International Understanding* itself, it is concerned more with peoples than with governments. However catastrophic the fortunes of war and politics, the very nature of a people and the essential conditions of their geography do not change. Who then are the Hungarian people? What is the nature of their country? How do they gain their livelihood? What is the social structure of the nation, its spiritual loyalties, the prevalent ideas in the.minds of the people and the origins of them?

WHO ARE THE MAGYARS? The name of Hungary in its own language is Magyarország—Magyarland; and its story and its problems are to a quite peculiar degree those of the strange and interesting people who inhabit it and to whom it owes that name. The Magyars are not, by origin, Europeans in the ordinary sense of the term. Their remote ancestors were a primitive tribe, distantly related to the Finns. Finnish and its cousin Estonian, are the only languages spoken in Europe to-day which bear any likeness to Magyar, and the Magyars always feel a warm sympathy for the Finns, as their nearest relatives. The forefathers of the Magyars, however, lived in ancient times far eastward of the present Finland, on the eastern slopes of the Ural Mountains. Here they mingled with nomad tribes who were roaming the plains of Central Asia, and under their leadership they journeyed by gradual stages across South Russia and the Ukraine, driven ever westward by the pressure of other nomadic races from the East. At last, at the end of the ninth century—that is over 1000 years ago—they crossed the Carpathian Mountains and pitched their tents on the further side, in the land which their descendants still inhabit.

THE MOUNTAIN-GIRDED PLAIN. The country in which they settled is a wide plain formed by the middle course of the Danube. The plain, with the inner slopes of the mountains which surround it, forms an area over 100,000 square miles in extent, and roughly circular in shape. In the west the open country is bounded by the Austrian Alps; in the south, by the mountains of Bosnia and Serbia; while the north and east are enclosed by the vast sweep of the Carpathians. Of these ranges, those of Austria and the Balkans are comparatively low and open—more 'mountain systems' than continuous ranges—and are able to support fairly large populations. These peoples—the Germans of Austria and the Slavs of the Balkans—were able to resist the invaders. Thus on these two sides the frontiers of 'Hungary', when they became established, did not extend beyond the foothills of the mountains. The main crest of the Carpathians, on the other hand, forms a wall broken by only a few passes. It is thus difficult to cross the mountains from north and east, while easy to approach them up the many valleys, nearly all of which converge on the central plain. Thus the Magyar invaders found it easy to conquer the sparse population of these highlands, and up to 1918 the frontiers of Hungary in the north and east ran along the central watershed of the Carpathians. Hungary thus included not only what, since 1918, has been the eastern half of Czechoslovakia (Slovakia and Ruthenia) but also in the east the much-disputed province of Transylvania, which after 1918 became Rumanian.

THE AGE OF CONSOLIDATION. Hungarian history since the 'Conquest' falls into two sharply distinct periods, divided by the central date of 1526. The first period was one of consolidation and progress. At first the new arrivals had to fight hard for their existence and independence against the Germans, who organized against them the 'Eastern March' of Austria, the old name of which Hitler revived in 1938. They survived this struggle, however, and in A.D. 1000 became one of the European family of nations, when their great king, St Stephen, great-grandson of the original 'leader' Árpád, who had brought them into Hungary, adopted Latin Christianity for himself and his nation, receiving from Pope Sylvester II the famous Holy Crown of Hungary. St Stephen's descendants and successors, the Hungarian kings of the eleventh and succeeding centuries, gradually made good their position. The nation multiplied, losing as it did so (partly through inter-breeding with neighbouring peoples) some of its wild, nomadic characteristics. The Magyars ceased to live in tents and built towns, churches and monasteries. From their primitive life of nomadic stock-breeders they became settled agri-culturalists. At the same time, the old social organization dissolved, gradually giving place to a new order which in many respects resembled that of all the European nations of the day, the English included. Round the king grew up an aristocracy of great nobles; at the other end of the scale, the peasants sank into bondage. The chief difference as compared with England was that the class of 'small nobles' or freemen were usually more suc-cessful in asserting their rights against the great oligarchs, so that the privileged class was larger. In consequence the class below them, the peasants, had a heavier burden to bear. Nevertheless, the nation flourished. During these centuries it ranked as a Great Power, preserving its independence against the German princes and intervening in Balkan affairs. The days of its great kings, Louis the Great (who also wore the Crown of Poland) and Matthias Corvinus, are remembered as the golden age of Hungarian history.

All this time, however, Hungary had to face a constant threat from invaders, pressing down from the east, along the same road taken centuries earlier by the Magyars themselves. The Tatars or Mongols devastated the country in the thirteenth century, wiping out a large part of its population. After them came the Osmanli or Ottoman Turks, who gradually conquered Asia Minor, Constantinople and the Balkan States. Against them the kings of Hungary waged almost constant defensive warfare from the fourteenth century onward, a struggle in which Hungary won the title of Shield and Bulwark of Christendom.

CONSEQUENCES OF THE TURKISH CONQUEST. This long blood-letting exhausted the Magyars and in 1526, at the famous battle of Mohács, in South Hungary, the Hungarian army was annihilated and its king perished. The victorious Turks now advanced and occupied all Central Hungary. For 150 years a Turkish Pasha ruled in Buda. In Transylvania native princes preserved a half-independence, while acknowledging the Sultan as their suzerain.

When this happened, the old native Árpád

dynasty had already died out in the male line 200 years previously. When King Louis II perished at Mohács, the Archduke Ferdinand Habsburg of Austria claimed the succession to the throne both of Hungary and Bohemia, of which Louis had also been king. Although the part of Hungary over which the Habsburgs could rule was only a strip of its northern and western edge, the acquisition of it, with that of Bohemia, enabled them to build up their dominions into the greatest of the Continental Powers.

For almost exactly 400 years Hungary remained part of the Habsburg Monarchy. At the end of the seventeenth century, the old frontiers were recovered, the Turks being driven out and Transylvania reincorporated soon after. But the new Hungary was only a shadow of the old. The Turkish rule had afflicted half the country with a desolation the effects of which are still visible today. Moreover the Magyar population of the central plains, which had been directly under the Turks, had been largely wiped out; whereas the Turks had done no more than raid the Slovaks and Ruthenes of the north, the Germans of the western fringe, and Transylvania, with its mixed population in which Rumanians formed a large element. The numbers of non-Magyars in Hungary were further increased, after the expulsion of the Turks, by immigration from the south of Serb and Croat fugitives from Moslem rule, and by the colonization of the unoccupied land. For this purpose settlers were brought in from all over Europe; but most of them were Germans, coming from South Germany and called by the people—as their descendants still are—'Swabians'. Thus by the eighteenth century the Magyars were in a minority in Hungary, and formed the largest element only in the central plains: the surrounding parts of the kingdom were inhabited in majority by other peoples, Germans, Slovaks, Ruthenes, Rumanians, Serbs. In the south-west, the population of Croatia, which was not an integral part of Hungary, although the king of Hungary had since 1102 worn the Crown of Croatia, had moved northward, since the Turks retained their hold of the mountainous south. The new Croatia now reached up to its present frontier, the Drave river.

THE RULE OF THE HABSBURGS. Though the Habsburgs had to leave Hungary most of the forms of its constitution, at heart they regarded it as a rebellious and unsatisfactory province. Their real aim was to weld all their dominions into a single, centralized, unified monarchy, over which they were to rule absolutely. These efforts led to many rebellions by Hungarians; the leaders of these, Bocskay, Rákóczi (after whom the famous Rákóczi March is named) and others, are still the national heroes of Hungary. The last great conflict, in 1848–9, was led by Louis Kossuth. The Austrian Emperor, Franz Josef, only put the rising down with great difficulty and had to call on Russian help to do so. Thirteen of its leaders were shot at Arad. They are remembered as the martyrs of Arad', and the anniversary of their execution is kept as a day of national mourning. Kossuth's name is still the most famous in Hungary as symbolizing her eternal struggle for liberty and independence. It is also revered by the peasants, since it was through his efforts that they received their liberty in 1848, when the relics of the medieval serfdom were abolished.

Actually, the result of the 1848–9 conflict was more of a compromise than appeared at first. The emperor was unable to make his despotism permanent and, in 1867, had to make his peace with the Hungarian leaders. The Habsburg dominions were reorganized as 'Austria-Hungary', and in them, under the new 'Dualist' form of state, Hungary had full freedom in her internal affairs and an equal voice with Austria in matters of common interest to both (chiefly foreign policy and defence).

DISRUPTION OF THE DUAL MONARCHY. This arrangement lasted almost exactly 50 years, but it broke down at the end of that period, chiefly because of its failure to give satisfaction to the aspirations of the 'nationalities' in both Austria and Hungary: that is, to the peoples other than the Germans in Austria or the Magyars in Hungary. So far as Hungary was concerned, although half the population was now non-Magyar, the whole form and spirit of the state was rigidly Magyar. The other peoples were, as inferiors, treated with much galling contempt and intolerance, and abused as traitors if they resented this treatment. The only result was, of course, to make them really discontented and very soon many of them were regarding Hungary as a prison and waiting their chance to join their brothers in the new national states which were growing, or which the future promised outside the frontiers of the Hungarian kingdom, namely, Serbia, Rumania or the Czecho-Slovak State, for which the Czechs were working in Austria. To this were added social discontents at conditions which, in some respects, were being modernized too quickly while in others they remained medieval. The end of the ancient Hungarian kingdom, in its old form, came after Austria-Hungary had fought the losing war of 1914–18. The national minorities received their freedom and set up their own states. Under the Treaty of the Trianon (1920), Hungary was reduced to the central core of the old kingdom. Of this the inhabitants were almost entirely Magyar. In area it was less than 30 % of the former territory, and included rather less than 35 % of what had been the kingdom's population. The remainder of the country was partitioned among the neighbouring states.

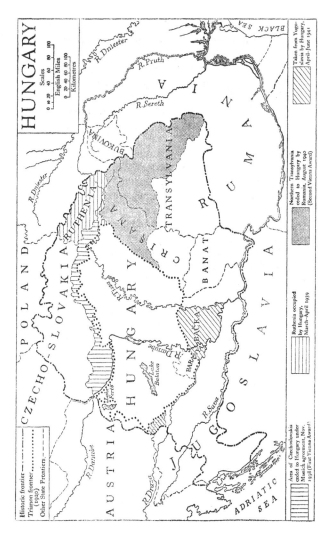

HUNGARY

Scales
English Miles
0 10 20 40 60 80 100
0 20 40 60 80 100
Kilometres

Historic frontier ——————
Trianon frontier ....
(1920)
Other State Frontiers — — —

Area of Czechoslovakia
ceded to Hungary under
Munich agreement, Nov.
1938 (First Vienna Award)

Ruthenia occupied
by Hungary,
March–April 1939

Northern Transylvania
ceded to Hungary by
Rumania, August 1940
(Second Vienna Award)

Taken from Yugo-
slavia by Hungary,
April–June 1941

Map labels: BLACK SEA · R. Dniester · R. Pruth · R. Sereth · BUKOVINA · BESSARABIA · POLAND · CZECHO-SLOVAKIA · RUTHENIA · TRANSYLVANIA · RUMANIA · CRISANA · BANAT · BACKA · BARANYA · HUNGARY · AUSTRIA · JUGOSLAVIA · R. Danube · Lake Fertö · Lake Balaton · R. Save · R. Drava · ADRIATIC SEA

Frontier changes, 1919–1941

CHAPTER II

THE FACE OF HUNGARY, 1919–1940

Within the limits imposed upon Hungary by the Treaty of Trianon, the state consisted, roughly, of the central plains which had formed the heart of the old 'historic Hungary'. Strips of the plain were, however, assigned, mainly on account of the railways running through them, to all the neighbouring countries, except Austria, while north of Budapest Hungary retained some of the foothills of the Carpathians, which at that point run far south. German and Italian help since 1938 put the Hungarians in dubious possession once more of nearly all the plain, as well as of the mountains of Ruthenia and northern Transylvania. In this chapter, however, only passing reference will be made to what lies outside the Trianon frontiers.

VILLAGES OF THE GREAT PLAIN. The Hungarian plain has a character which is very much its own, and very different at least from anything in Western or Central Europe. It is also, in many respects, remarkably uniform to the eye: in whatever part of it the traveller may be, he cannot doubt for an instant that he is in Hungary. This uniformity is, of course, partly due to human agency. All the cottages, which are the homes of more than half the population of Hungary, are built, with local variants, on the same general pattern. All are one-storied—a house with more than one story practically does not exist in Hungary outside the towns and, even in the towns, the suburbs usually follow the village pattern. Nearly all of them are white-washed, a plain surface without ornamentation. (The Germans of the Danube valley like a yellow wash, the Slavs draw a band of blue above the earth level, the Rumanians often go in for gay frescoes.) Each of them stands, usually narrow end on to the street, in its own courtyard, with the stables and barns at the back. A verandah runs along the side which faces the yard. The village churches, too, are almost all of a pattern. Except in some of the towns, and in a few sheltered corners near the western frontier, all the older buildings were destroyed in the Turkish wars, and the village church to-day is practically always a plain yellow building of the eighteenth or nineteenth century, varying only in size or in the possession of one or of two bulbous towers.

THE COMMUNAL PASTURE AND POND. Common to almost all Hungary, too, are the grazing-grounds outside each village, with the typical 'Gémkut' or crane-well, standing above the trough at which the cattle are watered. The 'Gémkut' consists of a rough pole, twelve or fifteen feet high, and ending in a fork. In this is balanced another log, with a chain at each end. From one chain hangs a bucket, which is dipped into the well or trough, while the other is used, lever-wise, to raise or lower the bucket. Horses and cattle are driven out in the morning and grazed communally, often by dashing young men, who summon their charges from each courtyard by a great fanfare on peculiar long trumpets of traditional shape. The swine, even more numerous, are usually in charge of an older man, but he, too, has his trumpet and his special call; and horse, cow or pig knows without error not only which tune he must obey in the morning, but also into which courtyard he must turn in the evening as the cavalcade proceeds down the village street, its guardian behind it, in a great cloud of dust. Only the geese, which are entrusted to the charge of little girls (the story of the goose-girl at the well surely originated in Hungary) are not woken by special music, which they supply by their own cackling. The communal pasture outside each village and the huge pond in the middle of it, with its geese and ducks, are common to nearly every Hungarian village throughout the country.

NATURE OF THE SOIL. There is much uniformity, too, in the cultivation. Huge fields of wheat or maize meet the eye everywhere. Nearly all the Hungarian soil is of the same type; a porous loess, which hardens in the higher areas to a dusty limestone, and crumbles in the flats into a loose sand. Through this there run comparatively few rivers, although those few—the Danube, the Tisza and their tributaries—are large and very important for the life of the country. Apart from them, water does not run in small streams, but collects in lakes and ponds, large or small, whence it eventually soaks its way underground to join the rivers. Thus in the plain it is rare to find a spring on or near the surface; on the other hand, almost anywhere

that a well is sunk, it will find water sooner or
later. In a village it is common to find a well in
each courtyard, or alternatively, one between every
pair of houses, serving two families. This water is,
of course, apt to be stagnant, and the supply of
pure water to the villages is one of the great health
problems of Hungary. Budapest and the other
large towns have their own supply. Two of the
lakes, both in West Hungary—Lake Fertö, or the
Neusiedlersee, now cut in two by the Austrian
frontier, and Lake Balaton, are very large; Balaton
is, indeed, the largest expanse of water in Central
Europe. Both are, however, extremely shallow,
and it is possible in some places to wade out in
them for a couple of miles. The vegetation varies
little. The most familiar trees are the poplar, the
scrub-oak, and above all, the acacia, strictly
speaking, the false acacia. This tree was first introduced into Hungary a century and a half ago, on
account of its property in binding together light,
sandy soils, and has now spread all over the
country. There are many woods of it, and many
village streets are adorned by a double row of
these beautiful, feathery trees. In the hills there
are beeches, oaks and a few firs, and along the
rivers, huge willows, alders and aspens.

GEOGRAPHICAL DIVISIONS.   But with all this uniformity, there is still a considerable diversity
between the different geographical areas of Hungary. The ancient Magyars, looking at the country
from the place of their first settlement, between
the Danube and the Tisza, and taking as the
dominant features the rivers which were so im-

portant for their flocks and herds, divided it as follows. There was the 'Dunántúl', or 'country beyond the Danube', i.e. the part lying within the bend of the Danube, or West Hungary; the Észak, or north, more commonly known as the Felvidék or Upper District; the Alföld, or plain, between the Danube and the Tisza; the Tiszántúl, or 'country beyond the Tisza'—the plain east of the Tisza; the 'right bank of the Tisza', in the north-east of Hungary; Transylvania, and the 'corner between the Tisza and Maros', afterwards known as the Bánát. Later events gave to the triangle enclosed between the lower reaches of the Tisza and the Danube the name of Bácska, and more recently still the extreme north-east corner of Hungary—the Podkarpatska Rus, or Carpatho-Ruthenia of Czechoslovakia, received the name of Kárpátálja (the country at the foot of the Carpathians).

Of these, the Treaty of Trianon left Hungary with only the Dunántúl (slightly diminished), a small part of Észak, the northern and central Alföld, without the Bácska, and part of the Tiszántúl. For geographical purposes, there is no noticeable distinction between the two last named; and Trianon Hungary falls naturally into two main divisions: Western and Northern Hungary (the Dunántúl and the Észak) and the Great Plain (the Alföld and the Tiszántúl).

THE TWO HALVES OF TRIANON HUNGARY. This division is more than geographical; that is, the dividing line of the Danube has in the past given the two halves of Hungary separate histories, which have resulted in social, political and spiritual differences. The west was for some centuries a Roman province (as was Transylvania, for a rather shorter period), while Central Hungary was still the camping-ground of wild nomads, such as Attila's Huns. The west has always been more exposed to Western, and particularly to Austrian, influence and infiltration. Above all, a considerable part of the west escaped the Turkish conquest, remaining under the comparative shelter of the Austrian armies. One result of this was that, while nearly all Hungary accepted the Protestant Faith (chiefly in its Calvinist form) in the sixteenth century, the west and north were reconverted to Roman Catholicism under the Counter-Reformation. The feudal institutions imported from Austria struck deep roots only in the west, which became the home of vast estates owned by princely families. When the east was resettled in the eighteenth century, huge estates were founded there also, but there was more mobility and less permanence. In politics, the west is more 'legitimist', i.e. more attached to the Habsburgs, while the east is more 'nationalist'. This difference is expressed in the Magyar words 'labanc' and 'kuruc', of which the former is derived from an old term meaning an Austrian soldier, while the latter is a corruption of the word 'crusader'. The Calvinist of the Alföld regards himself as the true Magyar and despises the man of the Dunántúl as 'half a Swabian'. The west, returning the compliment, points out that only among its own hills and valleys has there been any degree of continuity of population. The inhabitants of the plains, it says, are some of them Turks, the rest immigrants. It is true that while in most of the west (the fringe assigned to Austria in 1920 excepted), the Magyars have been able to absorb the foreign influences which penetrated there, the plain has not yet had time to digest the enormous numbers of immigrants which poured into it from 1700 onward. The centre of it is, it is true, purely Magyar to-day, and it is here that the most characteristic forms of Hungarian national life are found. But in the south and east of it the Magyars never recovered the ground which they lost under the Turks, and in fact these areas were split off from Hungary in 1920 on the strength of their non-Magyar majority. Most of the north was, of course, detached for the same reason; here the Slovak and Ruthene peoples had had a continuous existence from early times, and the Magyars had never penetrated in large numbers, although the landowners and the officials had been Magyars, or had adopted the Magyar language and ways.

WESTERN HUNGARY. The Dunántúl is not only sheltered by the Danube from the east, its whole geographical position is less open than that of the Alföld. It is a plain, by comparison with the Alps or the Carpathians, and most of it is low-lying; but it is traversed by several ranges of considerable height, the most important of which, beginning in a series of curious isolated hills of volcanic origin north of Lake Balaton, runs in more continuity through the regions known as the Bakony Forest and the Vertes hills, and reaches the Danube above Buda. The Bakony is the only part of Trianon Hungary which contains any large forests. Up to a century ago it was famous as a haunt of 'betyárs' (highwaymen) and is still the wildest part of Hungary.

South of the Bakony lies Lake Balaton, the playground of Hungary, dotted with fishing boats and yachts and surrounded by villas and pensions. Thence to the Drave, which forms the frontier with Croatia, the country is green, open and undulating; the best part of Hungary for cattle and horse-breeding. To the east, near the Danube, rise a few more high hills, where Hungary's largest coal deposits are found. To the west, the country rises gradually, and becomes more tangled as it approaches the borders of Styria—one of the remotest corners of Hungary, seldom visited even by Hungarians, and preserving many ancient national characteristics and customs. Finally, in the north-west corner, the Rába, winding its way in many channels through a flat valley to join the Danube, forms an open space known as the 'Little Plain' (Kis Alföld).

All this country, although still somewhat primitive to Western eyes, bears the signs of ancient cultivation. There are many small towns, most of them founded by Germans (who long formed the chief urban class in Hungary) and some containing fine buildings of the seventeenth and eighteenth centuries, and in a few cases, of earlier date. Sopron (Oedenburg), near the Austrian frontier, Pécs, with its ancient cathedral and Esztergom with its modern one, and Székesfehérvár, the oldest capital of the country, are the most interesting. None of these towns, however, is big and most of the population lives in villages, usually of 3–4000 inhabitants. The village is usually composed of only three or four streets, sometimes only one. The little white cottages stand along it at regular intervals; only in old villages where families have multiplied and land is short, one site will contain three or four cottages crowded together. All the cottages are usually much of a size, except for the houses of the village priest, the school-master and the notary. The older cottages are built of sun-dried brick, and thatched; the newer ones are of fired brick, and often roofed with the uglier but more healthy material known as 'eternit'. Most villages also contain one or more larger houses, the houses of the local squires or, as they call themselves (by the English word) 'gentry'. Every third or fourth village boasts a larger 'castle', the seat of the local 'magnate', prince, count or baron so-and-so. Sometimes these 'castles' face right on to the village street; more often they are set back in rather dusty parks. Each has a portico in front of it, with a coat of arms carved on the architrave; but like the cottages, they are usually one-storied and, like them, usually end at the back in farm buildings.

West Hungary is a pleasant country, in places well wooded and, although no hedges divide the fields, the sunken, dusty farm tracks, like deep Devonshire lanes, are often enclosed with acacias which meet over the head. A reasonable rainfall comes from the west, giving good crops, and the southern slopes of the hills are clothed with vine-yards yielding a wine which is light (not so light as it seems) but very palatable. The country is essentially rural and the population has long been almost stationary; in many places, indeed, the peasants have, to the great but ineffectual concern of the authorities, aimed at having only one child in order to keep their holdings intact, for by Magyar custom a farm is divided equally among its owner's children on his death. The German colonists, on the other hand—the Swabians— pass on their heritage undivided, usually to the youngest son, while the remainder seek their fortunes in the towns. This is certainly one reason why the Swabians prosper more than the Magyars. Their superior neatness, diligence and sobriety is, it must be confessed, another and not less potent reason.

The Swabians are to be found in some strength in the Bakony region, in the south-east, near Pécs (a region devastated by the Turks, recolonized and known by the Germans as 'Swabian Turkey'), and on the very outskirts of Buda.

BUDAPEST. Buda itself, the western half of the twin capital of Budapest, was once a typical German-Hungarian town, although containing also a quarter, now demolished, which was the home of Serbian merchants. Here stood the old Royal Palace, the Cathedral and also the winter palaces of the Hungarian nobles. Later, the new palace and most of the new Government buildings, the Ministries, etc., were built there. Buda, before destruction overtook it, was still rather an old-fashioned place, administrative rather than commercial or industrial. It stands on a steep hill, with a fine outlook over the Danube, Pest and the great plain beyond. Behind Buda hill, the wooded valleys were covered with modern villas, the homes of civil servants and clerks.

Pest faces it. It had a fine façade of fashionable hotels and cafés. Behind these the great city stretched out, first in a dense commercial quarter, then in an endless string of dreary factory suburbs. The whole city, including the satellite towns of 'Greater Pest', had a population of well over a million. It had some fine modern buildings, as well as some very ugly ones, but little that was worth seeing.

THE ALFÖLD. Beyond the outskirts of Pest begins the Alföld—the Great Plain proper of Hungary, an enormous expanse cut in two by the sluggish waters of the Tisza, but possessing few other natural features and, in the main, as flat as Norfolk. It is the home of everything that is commonly regarded as most characteristic and most romantic in Hungarian life. On its empty horizons the Fata Morgana (the Hungarian 'délibab') dances when the sunshine is hot. On such of the empty spaces as have not yet been put under the plough, the old Hungarian life may still be seen. Enormous herds of the ancient Hungarian cattle, which tradition avers the old Magyars to have brought with them from the East—lean, grey beasts, with huge horns and dark, gentle eyes—roam the plains in the charge of wild cowboys (*csikos*) in elaborate sheepskin cloaks. There are plains where the great bustard breeds and marshes haunted by the stork, the crane, the egret and all manner of exotic wild fowl. But in the main, the old life is dying out; where it is still preserved, as on the famous Hortobágy, west of Debreczen, it is chiefly as a museum piece, for the benefit of tourists. Most of the country has been brought under normal cultivation.

As such, its aspect—even apart from the mono-
tony of the landscape—is less attractive than that
of West Hungary. The effects of the Turkish rule,
which turned populous cultivated areas into deso-
late wastes, are still visible. The survivors from the
villages ravaged by the Turks took refuge in the
towns such as Szeged, Debreczen, Kecskemét,
Szabadka or Hódmezövásárhely, which swelled
into enormous conglomerations, villages on the
huge scale, each with one or two larger buildings
in its centre and round them miles and miles of
straight village streets, muddy in winter, dusty in
summer, lined with row after row of uniform, white
one-storied cottages. Between one town and its
neighbour, perhaps 30 miles distant, the whole
countryside would be left empty. Gradually, as
security returned, the people ventured out. At
first they built only rude shelters, *tányas*, in which
the men passed the summer, returning in winter
to the towns, where they had left the women,
children and old people. Presently the *tányas*
were made permanent and developed into regular
farms, so that in this part of Hungary there are
no villages, but only the few great towns and
between them the scattered *tányas*, whose isola-
tion is rendered more complete by the almost impossible state of the roads in spring and autumn.

The climate, too, is unfriendly. The summer is
often exceedingly dry, and the whole country
seems then to dissolve into a cloud of dust. On
the other hand, the spring, when the snows melt
in the mountains where the Tisza and its tributaries
have their head-waters, often brings disastrous
floods which cover the fields and sweep away the

flimsy mud-built houses. It is only recently that the work, not only of regulating the rivers against flood, but of irrigating the plains against drought, has been seriously undertaken. With modern methods an intensive cultivation, in particular of fruit trees, was begun. Through it some centres, such as Kecskemét, have achieved considerable prosperity.

THE BOUNDARY HILLS. The plain is bounded by hills. In the south the plain reaches right down to the frontiers of historic Hungary, and the first hills are those of Serbia. In the north, however, the Trianon frontier still left Hungary a certain amount of hilly country. This comes down close to the capital itself north of Budapest; indeed, the Danube runs here through what is almost a gorge, with the ruins of old castles overhanging it. East of Budapest the plain reaches further north, but there are still considerable hills, the summits of which are covered with beech forests and their lower slopes with vineyards. Here, too, are some noteworthy towns: Miskolcz and Diosgyör, centres of industry, and Eger, seat of an archbishopric, with the remains of an old Turkish fortress and a Turkish minaret still to be seen. Beyond this again comes another group of isolated hills, which produce the famous Tokaj wine, the richest and most powerful of all the Hungarian wines, of which it is said that it is 'the king of wines and the wine of kings'.

The mountains which enclose the Alföld on the east are those which form the boundary of Tran- sylvania, a great table-land encircled north, east

and south by the bend of the Carpathians. This
is not the place to describe this province, which was
transferred from Hungary to Rumania in 1920.[1]
It is a wild and fascinating country, full of high
mountains and wild forests in which bears, wolves
and lynxes still lurk, and inhabited by three races:
the Rumanians, who form the majority, the Magyars and the Germans or 'Saxons'. These last are
the people whom Browning alleges to be the
descendants of the children wiled away from
Hamelin by the Pied Piper. In actual fact, they
are the descendants of colonists from the Rhine-
land, who came here, on the invitation of Hungarian kings, many centuries ago. Their neat
prosperous villages and little walled towns form a
curious contrast to the picturesque but untidy
Rumanian hamlets or the ancient and dilapidated
castles of Hungarian nobles.

[1] See British Survey Handbook No. 2, *Rumania*.

CHAPTER III

THE ECONOMY OF HUNGARY

**RELATIVE IMPORTANCE OF AGRICULTURE AND IN-
DUSTRY.** Hungary is still mainly an agricultural
country, although not to such an extent as the
countries east and south of it—Rumania, Yugoslavia or Bulgaria—in which 70–80 % of the population still consist of peasants. Trade, industry
and town life have been developing fairly rapidly
during the last decades, and about 40 % of the
population now live in towns.

Nevertheless, the last occupational census taken
in Trianon Hungary showed nearly 52 % of the
population still engaged in primary production
(agriculture, forests and fisheries), against 23 % in
mining and industry, 5·4 % in trade and finance,
3·9 % in communications, the other 15·7 % being
divided between the public services, the professions, rentiers, domestic servants, etc.

Agriculture is not only the occupation of the
largest section of the population, but is also from
other points of view the most important item in
Hungarian economy. The exports still consist
mainly of agricultural products, raw or processed.
This has in recent years been felt to be a danger,
owing to the uncertainty of the harvest and the
low prices which have often obtained for agricultural produce. It has been largely for that reason—
although partly also with the object of absorbing
the surplus rural population, and partly for reasons

of national self-defence—that industrialization has been encouraged. The Hungarians themselves now claim that their country occupies a middle position between the industrialized West and the agricultural East. To the latter it exports, in normal times, a certain amount of industrial products in return for industrial raw materials, oil, and the few agricultural products in which it is not self-supporting. The chief of these is maize for fattening livestock. Hungary's exports to the West, however, are still overwhelmingly agricultural and imports from the West almost entirely industrial.

PRINCIPAL CROPS. Of the agricultural products, wheat is still by far the most important, especially for the export trade; whether Hungary is well or badly off in any given year still depends largely on the quantity and quality of the wheat harvest and the price of wheat on the world market. July, when the wheat is being reaped and threshed, is the climax of the year, when it is difficult to get Hungarians to attend to any other business whatever. A good deal of rye, barley and oats is also grown, rye being largely used for bread and barley for feed or brewing. In August the fields are full of maize, which is chiefly used for fodder but is also eaten on the cob. Potatoes and roots are becoming more important. Hungarians do not eat many fresh vegetables, and leave market gardening, except for onions, mainly to immigrant Bulgarian gardeners. Lately, however, the cultivation of fruit has made much progress, especially in the sandy districts of the Alföld. There is a considerable export trade in fruit, raw, pulped or canned; from some fruits, especially peaches and apricots, excellent liqueurs are distilled. In recent years, largely under the pressure of military necessity, the cultivation of industrial crops has made much progress.

THE VINEYARDS. Wine is produced in almost all parts of Hungary, often in very small peasant vineyards and by rather primitive methods. It is said that one family in every four of the entire population owns a vineyard. After the wheat harvest, the vintage is the great month of Hungarian agriculture, when half the population is out of its houses, gathering the grapes and pressing them in the tiny whitewashed huts which each family owns in its vineyard, perhaps a mile or so out of the village. The finer wines, which are exported, are cultivated in larger vineyards owned by the Crown, monasteries, or big landed proprietors.

LIVESTOCK. Livestock was at one time even more important than wheat, which only in the last century replaced cattle as the chief produce. In recent years, stock-breeding has regained a good deal of its importance and Hungary has now a large population of cattle and swine. Hungarians are rather heavy meat-eaters, even the poorer classes consuming a lot of bacon and lard. There is also a big export trade in cattle and pigs, live and slaughtered, and in various animal products, such as hides and bacon. Horses are bred for draught purposes, and the finer breeds also for sport. Sheep are bred less extensively: Hungarian wool is not of high quality, and the population does not take kindly to mutton as a dish.

Poultry, including geese, are kept on a very extensive scale. Of all aspects of a Hungarian village that likely to impress the traveller most vividly is that of the enormous numbers of snowy geese strutting about the street, splashing in and round the goose-pond in the centre of the village, or feeding in slow-moving flocks on the village green. The peasants rarely eat poultry themselves, but fatten them for the town market or for export. A considerable and growing trade is done also in poultry products, such as eggs and feathers.

INDUSTRY: EFFECT OF FRONTIER CHANGES. The oldest Hungarian industries are those connected with the processing of agricultural products: flour-milling, brewing, distilling, tanning, etc.; also industries working with local raw materials and for local consumers, such as brickworks. These are still among Hungary's most important industries, and have lately been reinforced by the development of the canning, pulping and kindred industries. Flour-milling, on the other hand, which had developed before 1914 to serve the entire Austro-Hungarian monarchy, passed through a severe crisis after 1918.

In the last decades before 1918, an effort had been made to develop Hungarian industry on a national basis. This was planned in accordance with the raw materials which Hungary then possessed. The factories engaged in primary production were sited near the sources of raw materials; the finishing industries were largely concentrated in and round Budapest.

The Treaty of the Trianon detached from Hungary a large part of her sources of industrial raw materials—in particular, far the greater part of her timber—with the factories sited near them, while leaving the bulk of the finishing industries inside the new frontiers. The only important raw material of which the majority was left inside Trianon Hungary in 1920, was coal, the chief mines of which were near Pécs, in Southern Hungary.

Hungarian industry was thus largely back in its old position of dependence on imported raw materials, which had to be paid for with the proceeds of exported agricultural produce. Something was done to remedy this by developing further local raw materials. The most important of these is bauxite, of which Hungary possesses very large deposits. Oil was also discovered near the Croatian frontier, and a not inconsiderable production was developed. In other cases, however, almost the whole of the materials had to be imported. These industries have suffered severely since the outbreak of war.

According to recent figures, the industrial group employing the largest number of hands (nearly 64,000), was the textile. After that came the iron and metallurgical industry, with 50,000, the machine industry with 40,000 and the foodstuffs industry with 34,000; the value of the production of this last group was much the highest of all. Other works employing a considerable number of hands were the glass and chemical industries, those utilizing wood and bones, the brickworks and the tanneries.

SMALL COMMERCIAL INCOMES. The whole structure of Hungarian life is still much simpler and less highly developed than that of a Western country. Moreover, Hungary has little carrying or transit trade, since the materials which pass across her territory between Germany and the Balkans require little transhipping or handling en route. Thus a much smaller proportion of the population is engaged in trade or banking than in England and the proportion occupied in providing pleasures or amenities is also small. The armed forces and the civil services, of course, have taken their share of manpower. Outside the very small class of great landowners, and an equally small group of big bankers and industrialists, few Hungarian families have been able to accumulate much money, and few Hungarians are able, or care, to save much during their working life. Thus the class, which is so numerous in England, of well-to-do families living on the capital accumulated by their forefathers, is almost entirely absent in Hungary. There were, indeed, a great number of pensioners after 1920, when the Government gave pensions to the civil servants evicted from the successor states. But what the Government could afford them was little enough. They are dying out, and their children are at work.

CHAPTER IV

THE SOCIAL STRUCTURE OF
THE COUNTRY

1. *The Countryside*

In spite of the industrialization of recent decades, the economic and social life of Hungary is still built up round its agriculture, and its most important problems are still those of its agricultural population. Those problems are also the most difficult; for whereas industry, when it began to develop in the nineteenth century, was able to make something of a clean start, agriculture was burdened with a heritage of medieval traditions and vested interests.

UNEQUAL DISTRIBUTION OF LAND. The agrarian population of Hungary still lives under conditions which differ, to their disadvantage, from those prevailing in most other countries. Its friends, who are few, call the system 'patriarchal', while its enemies, who are many both inside and outside Hungary, describe it as 'feudal'.

In the strict legal sense, the term feudal is inaccurate, since the inequality before the law and the restrictions of the personal liberty of the peasant, which existed in Hungary, as almost everywhere on the Continent, up to the nineteenth century, were abolished in 1848. If, however, the word is used in a broad sense, it is not an unfair description of rural conditions in Hungary, the most striking feature of which is the unequal distribution of the land. Nearly one-third of the whole area of the country consists of big estates and is in the hands of a small group of great landowners. The biggest of these, Prince Eszterházy, still owns something like 150,000 English acres, and estates of 20,000, 30,000 or 50,000 acres are not uncommon. Another quarter of the country is taken up by large and comfortable medium-sized farms, the houses, for the most part, of the 'lesser nobility' or 'gentry' as the Hungarians call them, corresponding to the 'squire' of the village, or else of yeoman farmers, usually of Swabian origin. Another quarter again is in the form of small farms whose occupants, the real peasants, are just able to get out of them a living for themselves and their families. The remaining sixth has been divided and sub-divided into a vast number of tiny holdings which are no longer able adequately to support their owners, who constitute the majority of the agricultural population. Below this class of 'dwarf-holder' there comes a great mass of population, the 'rural proletariat' which owns no land at all.

REGIONAL DIFFERENCES. These proportions of a third, a quarter, a quarter and a sixth are not, indeed, uniform throughout the country. The stronghold of the big estates is West Hungary, where the 'feudal' system has been able to develop unchecked throughout the centuries. Here, too, the population was not reduced by the Turkish wars, and the sub-division of the peasant holdings was already going on in the seventeenth and eighteenth

centuries. In the Great Plain, which was largely
resettled after the Turkish wars, the proportion of
yeoman farmers is much higher, and in the south
and south-east, where the landlord class was wiped
out altogether in the wars and the country completely recolonized, most of the population consists
of peasant free-holders. These are, however, very
largely Germans, the descendants of colonists
brought in by the Habsburg Emperors. It is a
little-known but important fact that of all the
nationalities in the old Hungary, it was the Magyars
among whom the largest class of 'landless proletariat' was to be found. Thus, even if the landlords
in the territories left to Hungary by the Treaty of
Trianon had not successfully resisted the reforms
carried through against their class in the areas
assigned to Czechoslovakia, Rumania and Yugoslavia, conditions in the contracted kingdom would
still have been particularly difficult. As they did
resist any large-scale reform, those conditions have
to-day reached a stage of acute crisis. A small
measure of land distribution was indeed carried
through in 1920, but on quite an inadequate scale.

PROPORTION OF LANDED TO LANDLESS. According
to a census taken in 1935, four and a half million
people in Hungary were then 'engaged in agriculture'. Of these, about one-third owned or leased
enough land to support themselves and their
families. These ranged from the great landowners,
with their thousands or even tens of thousands of
acres, through the small country gentlemen or
prosperous yeoman farmers, down to the smallholders who could manage to make ends meet.

Another third owned or leased some land, but had to make up their earnings from it by work during part of the year. They were thus in fact living below the poverty line. The remaining third had nothing at all. Some of these landless men are farm-hands working on big estates, in some cases with regular jobs which gave them a living. A farm-hand in Hungary is hired by the year, usually in March, and sometimes, of course, stays on the same estate all his life. Others depend entirely on casual labour, or on seasonal labour during the harvest months, for which they often hire themselves out in regular gangs, receiving the bulk of their pay in the form of a share of what they reap or thresh: this they take home to their families who live on it, through the winter months.

THE WORKING OF THE LARGE ESTATES. It must be explained that the big, and even the medium estates in Hungary are usually worked as units. The division of them into smaller leaseholds, let to tenant farmers, which is so common in the British Isles, hardly exists in Hungary. The chief exceptions are found on the huge municipal estates which belong to some of the towns of the Great Plain, and to a lesser extent, on some of the estates belonging to the Bishops and Religious Communities. Otherwise, each single estate is farmed as a single concern by the owner, with the help of managers and bailiffs, if it is large enough, and all the persons employed on it are in the position of labourers, although each of them often is given a little allotment for himself, as part of his wages. The big operations of reaping and threshing, etc. are done centrally. Many big owners, of course, own several estates, and often lease some of them.

Manual labour is very extensively used, even on the largest estates, which employ many more labourers than modern farms of the same size in England and, correspondingly, fewer machines. This is partly due to habit, partly to shortage of capital which has prevented the landlords from buying machinery. But it is also due to deliberate government policy; for the landlords were encouraged to go on using manual labour in order to save the farm-hands, for whom no alternative employment could be found, from falling into complete destitution. This policy was necessary, since there was not enough industry to absorb the surplus people from the land, but it naturally added to the difficulties of Hungarian agriculture, since, however low the wages that were paid, they yet formed a heavy charge on the landlord's balance-sheet. Since the outbreak of the present war, this had led to a new difficulty. Much of the labour has been drawn off for military service or by the needs of munition industries, but Hungary has not been able to manufacture, or to buy from Germany, the machines necessary to replace the old hand-labour. Agriculture has therefore, been suffering from a severe shortage of labour, which has affected the whole of production.

THE STANDARD OF LIVING. The living standards of the smaller peasants and of most of the agricultural labourers are extremely low. Their cottages look picturesque, but their walls of sun-dried brick, earthen floors and thatched roofs make them damp and unhealthy. The peasants eat very simply and the poorest among them, the seasonal labourers, are often literally half-starving during the months before harvest.

This can be paralleled in many other countries of Central and Eastern Europe, for in most of those countries all standards are far below those obtaining in Britain. Indeed, owing to the fertility of the Hungarian soil, even the poorest classes there still live better than the inhabitants of many other districts, especially those of the barren, rocky parts of the Balkans. In fact, the whole of Eastern Europe suffers from the same root evil of over-crowding on the land. In the past hundred years the population has increased very rapidly. While in Western Europe, when the same increase took place, the new industries were able to absorb the workers for whom there was no room on the land, in Eastern Europe, where capital was scarce, industry developed more slowly, and could only give employment to a small proportion of the growing country population. Before the last war there was a very large emigration to America from all the East European countries, including Hungary, but for the past twenty years the United States have admitted few immigrants. This is perhaps the chief reason why the position has continued to grow worse, although the falling birth-rate and the rather faster development of industry have brought some relief.

SOCIAL INFERIORITY OF THE PEASANTRY. Where the Hungarian small peasant or labourer is so much worse off than his Czech or Serb opposite number is in his social and political position. He belongs to an inferior class and is treated as such, and the whole machinery of the state has from time immemorial been organized to keep him in that position. Thus the demand for a real and radical land reform, which will certainly have to be satisfied in the near future, springs perhaps almost as much from the social and political causes, as from economic. Land reform would, indeed, substantially improve the condition of a considerable part of the rural proletariat, provided that, as well as being given land, they were fitted out to make an adequate start as independent farmers. But it would still leave behind quite a large class for whom land would not be available. For these room would have to be found in the towns, or overseas. Nevertheless, land reform would introduce a new, democratic spirit into Hungarian life, and in this spirit the further problems might be more easily solved. It is thus the indispensable first step, which must be taken before the rest can follow.

This is not to say that all Hungarian landlords are bad. Many of them, especially those which belong to families which are old without being rich—the old 'gentry' families—live in their villages modestly enough (for the average Hungarian landlord is far from being a rich man), caring for their dependents kindly and faithfully, and liked and respected by them. The system has its good side, as well as its bad. But it is a system of which both the good and the bad sides are out of tune, equally with the democratic ideas of to-day, and with the collective principle of the Soviet system.

It is clear that Hungary cannot emerge from the catastrophe of the present war without radical alterations of its country life.

THE MOVEMENT FOR AGRARIAN REFORM. There have, indeed, already been considerable changes in the last few years. Not only has the Government begun to take more interest in the villagers and farm labourers, but all Hungarian society has woken up to the fact that there was here a very neglected and miserable class, making up one-third of the whole population of the country. A group of young men went round the villages and described conditions, just as Charles Kingsley did for England a century ago, in a way which made everyone uneasy. The peasants and labourers themselves began to organize and to get into touch with other classes, particularly the socialists in the towns, and before March 1944, when the German occupation set everything back again, a strong political movement was growing up for land distribution, better conditions of work and more political freedom generally. The leaders of this movement were imprisoned by the Germans and their puppets; but, as soon as the latter were driven out, it was certain that the whole movement would spring up again and that no one would be able to stop it. In fact, the peasant leaders were prominent among the men who, as described below, set up a new government at Debreczen at Christmas 1944.

THE LIFE OF THE VILLAGE. Meanwhile, life in a Hungarian village is quiet enough. Where there is a 'big house', it is the centre of things, even for those villagers who are not the tenants or dependents of the landlord. Outside the 'big house', probably only the priest's and the schoolmaster's houses stand out a little from the rest. Even a big village may have no shop; the villagers buy what they need on their weekly visit to the local market town. There is, probably, an inn, but it is not much frequented, since each family makes its own wine. By day, during most of the year, the street is almost deserted; all the men are out in the fields, perhaps miles away. They come home in the evening, when the animals also are driven in, and for half an hour the whole place wakes up. Later, men and women sit on benches outside their doors, or in the street, under the acacias, smoking and talking. On Sunday they sit there all day, except when they are in the church.

It is a hard, monotonous life. It is monotonous even for the inhabitants of the 'big house', who are usually much poorer than they let anyone guess and often spend their lives with no bigger distraction than a little shooting or a drive over the bumpy mud roads to visit a neighbour, who is most likely also a cousin or a brother-in-law, five miles away. For the peasants, a wedding, a religious procession or a harvest festival are the great events of the year. A hard life, but not without its own charm. Few people know the Hungarian countryside. But if they do penetrate there, they will be received by landlord or by peasant, with much kindness and hospitality, and with the perfect courtesy and unfailing dignity which is equally the mark of the Hungarian gentleman and of the most ragged, barefooted Hungarian peasant.

2. *Urban Life*

THE TOWNS. While the life of the village or the
farm is still the most characteristic form of Hungarian life, it is no longer, as it was up to a century
ago, almost the only one. As has been said, 40 %
of the population lives to-day in towns. It is true
that many of the places which figure in the statistics
as 'towns' with quite large populations, including
Szeged and Debreczen, which rank respectively as
the second and third cities of Hungary, are of the
type described in chapter II, and except for
a few streets in the centre of each, they are really
only enormous villages; nearly the whole of their
population consists of peasants. Many of the other
towns are no more than small, sleepy country
markets. The only place which could claim to rank
as a great European city was still Budapest, which
was developed in the nineteenth century as the
capital of a country which then counted twenty
million inhabitants. Even after the reduction in
Hungary's size and population under the Treaty
of Trianon, it kept and even increased its lead,
since the smaller country needed no provincial
capitals. It was the seat of the Government and of
the entire central administration and the only important business centre in Hungary. With its
satellite towns east and south of Pest, which brought
the population of Great Budapest up to 1,300,000,
it was also by far the most important factory town.
The outskirts of Pest were, indeed, the only spot
in Hungary which bore any resemblance to a big
Western industrial town. Some of the provincial
towns, such as Györ, Pécs, Miskolcz, have industries

of some importance; but there is nothing in Hungary approaching a continuous industrialized belt or a 'Black Country'.

The Hungarian towns outside Budapest have not much to them. A few of them, particularly in West Hungary, have some nice old buildings, dating from the seventeenth and eighteenth centuries. Most of these towns were founded by German immigrants, and the population of them still spoke German until recent years. But in the main the Hungarian provincial town is a small, sleepy, rather slatternly place, which is still very much a part of the surrounding country. In the very centre there will be a few public buildings, a church or two, perhaps a hotel and may be a modern block of business offices. But in the side streets all the houses are one-storied, many of them standing in little gardens. The real centre of every town is its great market-place, in which, most mornings of the week, peasant women squat on the ground, surrounded by piles of fruit and vegetables or geese and poultry with their legs tied together. Once a week there is a larger market, to which the peasants come in from the whole countryside, distances of ten, fifteen or twenty miles. Then the whole square is packed with them, and with the little stalls on which the shopkeepers spread out the cheap goods, cloths, haberdashery or household implements, which they sell to the peasants. The real business of the week is done on market-day in the market; the peasant rarely enters a shop.

THE CAPITAL. Budapest was, so far as Hungary is

concerned, a world by itself. Although the country priests railed at its vices, nearly the whole nation was intensely proud of it, and its visitor is certain to be deluged with descriptions of its past beauties, mingled with lamentations over the dreadful sufferings inflicted on it as the tide of war has swept over it. Something has already been said of its beautiful situation on the two banks of the Danube: Buda, with its royal palace, its cathedral and its public buildings, stands on the high hill overlooking its western bank with wooded hills covered with villas and gardens, behind; Pest, sprawls out on the eastern bank, with vast suburbs running out onto the dusty Alföld. Half a dozen bridges linked the two, the most famous being the celebrated Suspension Bridge, built a century ago by the Scot, Adam Clark. The next above it, the Margaret Bridge, blown up in the autumn of 1944, gave access to the famous Margaret Island, the playground of the well-to-do of Budapest, with hotels, cafés, swimming baths, gardens and tennis and polo grounds.

Pest is the modern city, in which those who wanted it could find everything which a big modern town has to offer: shops, and restaurants, cafés and night-clubs, and also very excellent museums, picture galleries and libraries. Buda is much smaller and was quieter, but contained a multitude of small inns and restaurants with pleasant gardens, which were the favourite resorts of the people of Budapest.

The average Hungarian of the city took a great many of his meals in restaurants, and was fond of spending long evenings, especially in the summer, where it was possible to sit in the garden or courtyard, drinking a little wine, talking and listening to the gypsy orchestra. Both food and wine were cheap (and you were not expected to drink much); time was not expensive, and a small tip to the leader of the orchestra would bring bows and compliments as though you were a duke at least, and a selection of tunes played at your table, right into your ear. For other times of the day, particularly after the mid-day meal, which in Hungary is the principal meal, there were the cafés, where, again, you might spend all the time you had to spare at no more expense than the price of a cup of coffee. All cafés kept the newspapers, and the waiter would bring you any that you wanted. The big Budapest cafés, and the main cafés in the larger provincial towns, had foreign newspapers, including English, as well as Hungarian.

THE JEWS. Until a year or two ago, almost all the shopkeepers in Hungary were Jews. The true Hungarian, the Magyar of the upper and middle classes, despised business as a career not fitting for a gentleman. If, therefore, he could not live as a landowner, he entered the public service as a civil servant or officer or schoolmaster, or perhaps went into the Church. Even the poor man who saved a little money and wanted to better his son did not try to set him up in business, but got him a job in the police, or the railways, or in some small government office. Thus the middle classes of Hungary consisted of two worlds, living side by side and mixing very little: the Magyars in the government services the Jews in business, finance and most of the professions.

As everywhere in Central Europe, there were a great many Jews in Hungary. The last census showed about 800,000 Jews out of a total population of 14,000,000. There were over 200,000 Jews in Budapest alone. Outside the capital they were most numerous in the north and east, near the Polish frontier; but there was no town in Hungary without its Jewish colony, and even in a village of any size the village shopkeeper, most likely the innkeeper, perhaps the doctor and the vet, would be Jews. If there was a big estate, a Jew would probably keep its accounts.

Many of the Hungarian Jews had lived in the country for generations, spoke Magyar as their mother tongue, had taken Magyar names and had begun to intermarry with their Magyar neighbours. In the north-east, however, where many of the Jews were recent immigrants from Poland, they wore the traditional Jewish costume, spoke Yiddish and preserved their strict Orthodox religion and distinctive habits. On the whole, relations between Jews and Christians in Hungary were, until recent years, not bad. The two classes of society did not mix very much, but they lived fairly happily side by side. Nineteenth-century Hungary was, in fact, very proud of its 'liberalism' in admitting Jews freely into the country and in not discriminating against them; and its rulers were well aware that the Jews were developing the country economically in a way which they themselves would not have had the experience, or the capital, to do. There was, indeed, plenty of room for both classes.

GERMAN ANTI-SEMITISM. After the last war, however, there was a considerable reaction against the Jews, partly because the Communist leader Béla Kún, who ruled in Hungary for some months in 1919, and most of his leading assistants, were Jews. Furthermore, times were changing. There were no longer places enough to go round in the State service and the younger generation of Magyars began to look for business careers, and to regard the Jews as rivals. This affected especially a class of Hungarians who have played a very important and very disastrous part in recent history: the young generation of 'Swabians' (see Chapter 1). The sons of Swabian peasants who came to Budapest to make their living could not, like the son of the old Magyar aristocratic or 'gentry' family, reckon on influential family connections to get them safe jobs in some ministry. They had to make their own way in the world, and it was they, more than any other class, who felt the force of the Jewish competition. Then when Hitler and his Nazis came into power in Germany, the Swabians, in spite of their Magyar upbringing, and very often, Magyar names, suddenly felt themselves German. They not only sympathized with Germany's political aims, but also with the Nazi social ideas, including anti-semitism. They infected others, and before long there was a considerable party in Hungary clamouring noisily for the adoption of the Nazi system, and in particular for laws and measures against the Jews similar to those which the Nazis were enforcing in Germany.

The Hungarian government and people did not give way easily to this clamour. But it was not difficult to whip up a good deal of ill-feeling against the

Jews, particularly among the younger generation who found it difficult to get jobs, and resented the much greater wealth of the average Jew. Yielding to the popular demand, laws were passed restricting the proportion of Jews in the professions and universities and expropriating Jewish-owned land. But the Jews still enjoyed a degree of protection not paralleled in Nazi-controlled Europe until March 1944, the fatal date when the Germans really established control in Hungary. Then the gang of professional anti-semites came into power who introduced the counterpart of the Nuremberg laws into Hungary, with all their accompaniment of the ghetto, the yellow star, eviction from almost every job and every kind of brutal and humiliating restriction.

It was also established that the Jews, who had not been allowed to serve in the army and had been formed into separate labour corps, were being sent to Poland to work behind the German lines, and it was feared that they were being exterminated there by the Germans. This fate was reported to have been inflicted on all the Jews of Hungary outside Budapest, men, women and children alike. The deportations were stopped on the intervention of the Pope, the King of Sweden and others, but were renewed, and extended to Budapest, when the Arrow Cross seized power in October 1944.

The more progressive and decent elements in Hungary never approved of the excesses of the Germans and their despicable agents, and no doubt will be anxious to re-establish a humane and honourable relationship between Jew and Christian after the war. What form that will take it is difficult to say, for the events of 1944 have deepened the consciousness, even among those who repudiated the excesses, of the difference between the two races, and the problem of finding jobs for the younger generation of non-Jews is not likely to have become easier.

LIFE OF INDUSTRIAL WORKERS. About a quarter of the population of Hungary is employed in industry. The term covers all industrial processes, down to the village smith or carpenter, and nearly one-half of the persons listed as 'industrial workers', are in fact artisans or home-workers or employed in very small concerns with perhaps only one or two assistants. The government has always been anxious to encourage this smaller industry, both as a means of relieving rural unemployment and as constituting a social, dependable, God-fearing element of the population.

The other and greater half are the factory workers, employed in larger concerns with a payroll of ten or more. The most important of them are the great Manfred Weiss munition and metallurgical factories on Csepel Island, south of Budapest. There is a big iron works, belonging to the State, at Diosgyör, another munitions factory at Györ, and some sizeable textile factories in Budapest. Outside Pécs, there are local mines. All industry developed quickly after the outbreak of war, to meet the needs, not only of munitions, but of other supplies for the army.

The position of the industrial workers in Hungary is, on the whole a good deal more satisfactory than that of the workers in the villages. As in every country in the nineteenth century, the authorities were hostile to the idea of the workers organizing, and when they began to do so, tried to split the movement by setting up a 'national' centre, in which all the workers in State service, including the employees of the railways, had to belong. There were also Christian Trade Unions. But the Social Democrat Trade Union movement, akin to the British Labour movement, proved much the stronger, and although the Trade Unions were forbidden to engage in politics, they got round this by forming 'shadow' unions, to which each member of an official union belonged. Ever since the last war the Social Democrat Party has managed to win a few seats in Parliament. Like the Peasant leaders, the Social Democrat leaders stood up boldly during the present war for freedom and independence and openly opposed the Government's subservience to Germany. In 1943 and 1944, after they had concluded an alliance with the peasants' leaders, they were becoming a power in the land. In March 1944, the puppet government imprisoned them and placed the whole Labour movement under the 'national labour centre', afterwards introducing new single labour organization for the whole country. The workers' own leaders re-emerged to take a leading part in the Provisional Government established in the area controlled by the Red Army, in December 1944.[1]

[1] In the Miklós Government, responsible to the elected Provincial National Assembly at Debreczen, Agoston Valentini, a branch Secretary of the Social Democrat Party, became Minister of Justice, Dr Takats, also a Social Democrat, Minister of Industry, and Dr Molnár, of the same party, Minister of Social Services.

CONDITIONS OF LABOUR. Wages in Hungary are low compared to English standards, but higher than in Rumania or the Balkans. They are especially low for unskilled and female labour, whereas the skilled craftsmen, of whom there is a shortage, can command a fair price for their work. Collective bargaining exists, and wages are fixed for trades, varying between Budapest and the provinces. The cheapness of food and the fact that few workers have to live far from their place of work partly offsets the small money wage. In recent years a good deal has been done to improve general working conditions. The biggest gap is the absence of any system of unemployment assurance, or even of any organized relief. In other respects, however, social legislation in Hungary, for the industrial worker, compares not unfavourably with that of most countries at a similar stage of economic development. Since the last war a very modern system of sickness assurance was introduced. Shortly before the present war, old age, invalidity and dependents' assurance, Sunday rest and holidays with pay were introduced, and, after hours of work had come down rapidly by trades, the 8-hour day and 48-hour week were introduced in principle. When war broke out, the Government took powers to suspend all protective legislation, but did not use its powers widely, beyond introducing compulsory direction of labour in agriculture and in factories working on war production. A great deal of overtime was worked in some factories, but the legalized overtime rates were paid. Sunday rest and holidays with pay remained in force. The whole wage and price level was taken under government control, and the wages of industrial workers were raised rather more than those of others, such as government employees. The workers complained, however, that the rates were unreal as, owing to war shortage, many commodities of which the prices were nominally controlled, were actually unobtainable except on the 'black market', which was out of the working man's reach.

The Hungarian worker has certainly had a hard time during the war, especially since the German hold tightened; the more so as his sympathies were for the most part against his own government and against Germany. The English visitor, if he were able to communicate with the Hungarian workman (many of them speak some German, but few speak English) would find him a decent, self-reliant and friendly man, anxious to talk and exchange experiences and with a good deal in common with his opposite number from an English factory.

CHAPTER V

POLITICAL AND RELIGIOUS
INSTITUTIONS[1]

The political structure and institutions of Hungary
are in many respects very like those of Great
Britain—a fact which Hungarians are rather fond
of emphasizing. They like to recall that their Parliament is practically as old as ours, and that the
'Golden Bull', which thereafter formed the great
charter of liberties of the nobles, is only a few years
later than our own Magna Carta. The Parliament
buildings in Budapest were built in conscious
imitation of those in Westminster, and like them,
stand on the river bank.

There are, of course, many differences also, both
in the institutions themselves and still more, in the
spirit in which they are worked. It must never
be forgotten that a large part of Hungary was for
200 years under Turkish rule, which meant that
it was simply reduced to a desert. During this
time, most of the rest of the country, and the whole
of it for another 200 years afterwards, was ruled
by the Austrian Emperors, who were foreigners
and often at loggerheads with the Magyars. The
country has also had to suffer many wars and in-
vasions, which prevented conditions from becoming settled or trade and industry from developing. The great Industrial Revolution, which

[1] As they existed up to the time when the tide of war
swept over Hungary in 1944.

altered the whole face of England, never came to
Hungary at all until quite recently, and then it was
on a much smaller scale than ours, since Hungary
had neither the coalfields nor the shipping on which
the English factories flourished. Thus Hungary is
in many respects much more like England as it
was a century or 150 years ago than England as
it is to-day. It has, indeed, been changing very
fast in the last generation, especially during the
present war, but the very rapidity of the changes
has left it with many very difficult and unsolved
social problems.

CONSTITUTIONAL MONARCHY. Hungary is a constitutional monarchy, which in normal times possesses a king, a parliament and an extensive system
of local government. The Crown is, as it were, in
suspense at the present moment.

The last King of Hungary, Charles V, who was
crowned in 1916, left the country in 1918 and, after
two unsuccessful attempts to return to it, died in
1922. His eldest son, Otto, never entered Hungary. Hungarian constitutional tradition does not
recognize the king as in full possession of his rights
until the venerated Holy Crown has been placed
on his brow. Moreover, the confused happenings
which followed the last war enabled a party in the
country to argue that the old agreement, under
which the succession to the Crown belonged to
the Habsburg family, had lapsed. Finally, both
the Allied and Associated Powers and Hungary's
neighbours insisted that they could not allow a
Habsburg on the throne. Pending a settlement of
the question, Admiral Horthy was elected Regent

in 1920, and has held that office ever since.[1] In practice, the Regent exercises nearly all the rights of a crowned king, except that of creating titles of nobility, and some special rights connected with the Roman Catholic Church, which are vested in the crowned king of Hungary. His son has, however, no claim to succeed him, and Horthy's elder son, who might have done so, was killed during the present war, in mysterious circumstances, while flying on the Russian front.

PARLIAMENT. The Hungarian Parliament consists of two Houses, of which the Upper House is composed in part of representative peers, in part of ex-officio members, such as the heads of the various Churches, in part of representatives elected by the Counties and by various bodies (Chambers of Commerce, Industry, etc.) and in part of members nominated by the Regent. The Lower House is elected, but on a system which has always left it very unrepresentative of any except the upper and middle classes. Since 1920 the franchise has been secret in the towns, but until the elections of 1939, it was open in the country districts; and when, for these elections (from which the last Parliament emerged) the secret ballot was made general, the franchise was restricted. Moreover, no elections were held in the districts 'reacquired' by Hungary after 1938; for these, Deputies were nominated by the Government.

[1] In law: in fact he was supplanted by the Arrow Cross leader Szálasi who, with Nazi support, seized power when Horthy had broadcast the news that he had appealed for an armistice, on 15 October 1944.

The great bulk of the Deputies, ever since 1920, have belonged to a great central party, most recently known as the *Party of Hungarian Life*. There have been a certain number of Deputies representing the extreme Right—the *Arrow Cross*, the *National Socialists*, and a party known as the *Party of Hungarian Regeneration*. On the other side, there have been the small *Catholic Party* and a handful of *Social Democrats*, *Small-holders* and *Liberals*. The Szálasi Government installed by the Nazis in October, represented the domination of the quite discredited Arrow Cross; it repressed all members of the Centre as well as of the Left.

LOCAL GOVERNMENT.   For purposes of local government, Hungary is divided into Counties. Each of these has at its head an official nominated by the Government and called the *Föispán*—a title usually translated as Lord Lieutenant. Under him is the *Alispán*, or Deputy Lieutenant, a permanent official elected by the County. Each County has its own Council.

The 'County' is a characteristic Hungarian institution, with a long tradition of which it is very proud, and in the old days the Counties were very independent and often very powerful. To-day their influence is much smaller, since under modern conditions much of the administration is conducted centrally from Budapest, through the various Ministries; and many officials in various parts of the country are directly subordinated to their Ministry, not working through the County. The latter, however, still possess much wider powers than an English County Council.

Budapest and a few other large towns rank as Counties. Smaller towns have their own councils, but are subordinated to the County in which they are situated. Each County is also subdivided into rural districts, and these again into communes, which form the lowest grade of administration. Each commune, or village, has its own elected Council, but also a clerk or notary, who is an official of the County.

The police consists of two bodies: the gendarmerie for the rural districts, who are a military body, carrying firearms and wearing splendid feathered hats; and the ordinary police in the towns. The Nazi-controlled Government of 1944 began to 'militarize' the police also.

THE CHURCH.   The Church counts for a great deal in Hungarian life. On Sundays almost everyone living within reach of a place of worship goes to Mass or the Protestant service, as the case may be. Especially in the country districts, the religious ceremonies are the chief occasions of the year. A very characteristic sight in Catholic districts is a long procession, consisting of most of the population of an entire village, walking slowly along the road, led by their priests and carrying banners with religious symbols. This going in procession is known as 'Búcsú' (literally 'farewell').

Hungary is a country of mixed religions, among which the Roman Catholic has the largest number of followers and holds, in most respects, the leading place. As has already been told, Hungary was converted by the Western Church nearly 1000 years ago, and ever after considered herself as standing under the special protection of Rome.

This tradition is still alive, even in politics. The Holy See concedes to the King of Hungary, who bears the title of Apostolic King, special rights which it claims for itself in other countries, and has exercised its influence in favour of Hungary on many occasions. In return, the Catholic Church enjoyed a specially privileged position in Hungary up to modern times; and, although all the chief Confessions are to-day nominally equal, the Catholic Church is recognized as the senior among them. There are three Roman Catholic Archbishops of Hungary—the Archbishops of Esztergom, Kalocsa and Eger. The first-named, who is in fact always made a Cardinal, is the head of the Roman Church, and one of the most important figures in the country, particularly when, like the present Benedictine Archbishop, Cardinal Seredi, he is a commanding personality.

The Hungarian Succession Law provides that the King of Hungary, as wearer of the Holy Crown, must always be a Catholic. The chief national festival is St Stephen's Day (20 August), and the most venerated of all the national relics is the Holy Crown. Next to it comes the Sacred Right Hand of St Stephen, which was found preserved, in a mummified condition, about a century after the Saint's death, and is carried in procession every St Stephen's Day through Budapest with a dazzling array of gold-broidered vestments, uniforms and traditional costumes.

The Church is one of the largest landowners and

one of the richest institutions generally in Hungary. Besides the Archbishops and the Bishoprics, many of the monasteries have received vast endowments from kings and other pious persons. The leading order is the Benedictine, whose chief house at Pannonhalma, in West Hungary, is an 'Arch-Abbey', not subject to the jurisdiction of any bishop. The Cistercians, Franciscans and Piarists also possess many monasteries. All education in Hungary was in the hands of the Church up to modern times, and these four Orders still conduct a large number of secondary schools. A considerable proportion of the primary schools are also 'confessional', that is, parochial schools.

There is a rather wide gap between the higher and the lower Catholic clergy. The village priests are relatively poorly paid and have to live modestly. Nevertheless, they enjoy much esteem, and rightly, for they are a devoted and well-educated body of men.

THE PROTESTANTS. Considering the position held by the Roman Catholic religion, it may seem strange that the confession which is commonly regarded as the most 'national', and which is nick-named the 'Magyar faith', should be not the Catholic, but, on the contrary, the Calvinist. In the fifteenth and early sixteenth centuries nearly the whole country was converted to Protestantism, the German colonists and a few others adopting the Lutheran confession, while most of the Magyars followed the doctrines of Calvin.

In the seventeenth century West Hungary, which was then under the direct rule of the Habsburgs, was reconverted to Roman Catholicism; but Central Hungary, which was under the Turks, and Transylvania and the East, which were practically independent, resisted the 'Counter-Reformation'. Indeed, the Princes of Transylvania fought the battles of their co-religionists in West Hungary, and it was because neither party was strong enough to crush the other that toleration and equality between the main religions were established, first in Transylvania—the first country in Europe where this occurred—and later in the whole of Hungary. As the Habsburgs represented a foreign influence, Calvinism became linked with the idea of Magyar nationalism and Hungarian independence.

RELIGIOUS TOLERANCE. This distinction still exists, but politically and geographically Western and Northern Hungary are still overwhelmingly Catholic, while the plains of the Alföld are predominantly Calvinist: the chief Calvinist centre is Debreczen. In Transylvania, the Magyar population is partly Catholic, partly Calvinist, partly Unitarian.

Politically the Roman Catholics are still rather identified with the Habsburg cause, the Calvinists with the opposition to it. Socially, most of the great aristocratic families, except those of Transylvania, are Catholic, as are the peasants among whom they live, while the Calvinists are stronger among the 'gentry' and independent families. The old quarrels between the two Confessions have, however, died out. They live together in harmony and are on a footing of equality which is carefully preserved. The Protestants have perhaps in the last twenty-five years enjoyed a political influence out of proportion to their numbers, owing to the fact that the Regent and many of his special circle and advisers were Calvinists. Actually, in Trianon Hungary about 75 % of the population was Roman Catholic and 20 % Calvinist, and this represents roughly the proportion of the adherents of the two Confessions among the Magyars.

THE MINORITIES. A good many of the non-Magyars of Hungary are also Catholic or Calvinist; thus the Croats, most of the Slovaks and a fair proportion of the Germans are Roman Catholic.

But several of the non-Magyar peoples of Hungary belong to Churches which are distinctively theirs, or to which, at any rate, few Magyars belong. Nearly all the Ruthenes are Catholics of an Oriental Rite, or 'Uniates'. Of the Rumanians, some are Uniates, the remainder Orthodox; the Serbs are Orthodox. Many of the Germans are Lutherans. The only other important religion is the Jewish.

While the Uniate Church is a part of the Roman Catholic Church, the other Churches all enjoy almost complete autonomy, and thanks to the system of 'denominational education', which long prevailed extensively in Hungary, and still exists in large measure, the non-Magyars were able to exercise a degree of control over their own schools. This independence was, it is true, much reduced in the past fifty years, but it was certainly through their Churches that those non-Magyars who were neither Catholic nor Calvinist were able to preserve as much independence as they did. The non-

Magyars who were Catholic or Protestant 'assimilated' far more to the Magyars than did the Orthodox Serbs or Rumanians. As regards religion itself, tolerance prevails; and, although the non-Magyar churches are not so rich as the Roman Catholic, they have not to complain of their status. Only the Jewish question, which has been described above, stands out differently.

CHAPTER VI

INTERNATIONAL RELATIONS,
1919–1944

Many Hungarians are eager to express admiration
and even affection for Great Britain. They copy
many of our ways and they like to think that their
institutions, their outlook on life and their interests
resemble ours. These feelings are quite genuine;
and yet, in spite of them, Hungary has now been
involved in war with the British twice in a generation, at the side of their bitter enemy. What is
the reason for this?

THE GERMAN HUNGARIANS. First, although these
are the feelings of most of the population, they
are not those of them all. There is, as has been said,
a fairly strong German element in Hungary. If
those who still enter themselves as German-
speaking are less than 10 % of the population, and
they mostly peasants, there are perhaps almost as
many Hungarians again whose ancestors were
German and who, especially in the last ten years
or so, have come to feel more German than Hungarian. Many of Hitler's doctrines, and most of
all, undoubtedly his anti-Semitism, has made a
natural appeal to this class. Unfortunately while
the German-speaking peasants are without much
influence, these sons or grandsons of peasants, who
left the farms and secured a position in the national
life, are very influential indeed.

Many have climbed to the top in politics, in the government offices, in the Church, and above all, in the army, which, so long as Hungary belonged to the Austro-Hungarian Empire (in which the army was a central service under the direct command of the King-Emperor) was a career which Magyars tended to avoid as 'un-national'. In recent years the influence of the high army officers has been important, and Hungary's policy has been very strongly influenced by the fact that so many of them were of German blood.

FEAR OF THE SLAVS AND OF BOLSHEVISM. The people of German origin are not, of course, the only pro-Germans in Hungary. Many others, especially in the middle classes, have been infected by the same ideas, particularly by the anti-Semitism, and by admiration of the German army and belief, spread by clever German propaganda, in its invincibility. To this has been added, both in 1914 and above all, since Hitler attacked Russia in 1941, the Russian factor. The Magyars, in their lonely position encompassed north and south by Slavs, and with the huge Slav masses of Russia just across their frontiers, have always been terrified of the Slav danger.

Moreover, in 1918 and 1919 there occurred events which have left a deep mark on all subsequent Hungarian history. When the war was drawing to a close and the imminent defeat of the Central Powers was apparent, the old regime gave way and was replaced by a new government of the Left, friendly to the Entente, under Count M. Károlyi. This government proclaimed the separation of Hungary from Austria and subsequently proclaimed Hungary a Republic. Károlyi attempted to carry through social and democratic reforms, but the situation was too much for him. Rumanians, Czechs and Serbs were pushing into the areas claimed by them, economic distress was extreme and radical agitation grew. Eventually, in March 1919, Károlyi was supplanted by a Communist Government, in which the ruling spirit was Béla Kún, who also failed either to rally the country behind him or to stop the advancing armies of Hungary's neighbours. In the summer of 1919, Rumanian troops actually occupied Budapest— leaving behind them, when at last they were induced to retire, many bitter memories.

A 'White' Government had meanwhile been organizing outside the reach of the 'Red' regime. Their representatives now entered Hungary and established themselves as the legal Government. Before conditions had settled down they had carried through against their predecessors a 'White terror', which has never been forgiven them.

The men of this regime were by their own confession, and indeed, by their own boast, essentially 'counter-revolutionaries'. They ascribed to 'Bolshevism' every imaginable horror, and thus looked on Russia, as the seat of the Third International, with a double fear and loathing. Thus Hitler's denunciations of Bolshevism found a ready hearing among the ruling classes in Hungary, and they carried their country into war in 1941 cheerfully enough, under the impression that the victorious German army was not only going to destroy the Slav danger, but also to 'exterminate Bolshevism'.

Nor were the traditional ruling classes the only blind 'anti-Bolsheviks' in the country. The Arrow Cross, who seized power in October 1944 precisely because the Regent had agreed to seek terms in Moscow, were fanatic in their hatred of Bolshevism; and yet this movement, although not representative of the proletariat, was largely drawn from it.

THE LEGACY OF THE TURKISH OCCUPATION. The anti-Bolshevik element is quite modern, and applies only to the present generation. The other question, that of the 'Slav menace' is part of the larger problem which really settled which side Hungary would take, both in this war and in the last. Indeed, the whole position probably dates back to the blood-letting of the Turkish wars, from which, as has been shown, Hungary emerged with only the centre of her territory Magyar and with Slavs and Rumanians in the majority in the north, south and east. Distasteful and oppressive as the subsequent Habsburg rule was to Hungary, most Hungarians recognized that only Habsburg protection could save them from the Turks, and in more modern times, from other dangers: Russia, and the claims of Serbia and Rumania. In the last half-century before 1918, while this situation still existed, a new factor was introduced by the aspirations of the Slavs inside Austria itself. A federalization of Austria, as the Austrian Slavs desired it, might have kept the Monarchy intact but would inevitably have led sooner or later, to Hungary loosing her own Slav districts. Thus the Hungarian leaders found themselves bound not only to Austria, but to the centralist German element

in Austria, as the only racial element in that
country which did not threaten Hungary's terri-
torial integrity; for the Germans of Austria did not
interest themselves particularly in Hungary's German population.

THE BOND WITH AUSTRIA AND ITS CONSEQUENCES.
Although, therefore, in 1914 the leaders of Hungary genuinely did not want the war, self-preserva-
tion prohibited them from leaving Austria and Germany in the lurch, even if they had been able to
determine their own foreign policy, which was not
the case. Thus in 1918 they were inevitably left,
with the Germans of Austria, as the defeated enemy,
while the other nations of the Monarchy gained
their independence at the hands of the Allies,
forming, largely at the expense of Hungary, the
new States of Yugoslavia and Czechoslovakia, and
the greatly enlarged State of Rumania.

It is true that Austria also received some German-
inhabited districts in West Hungary, the Burgenland, but although Hungary bitterly resented
Austria's action in claiming these districts, as
treachery to her old partner, they were insignificant
compared to what was lost to the other States.
Moreover, there were only a few thousand Magyars
in the Burgenland, while Rumania, Czechoslovakia
and Yugoslavia each received, not only the districts
in which Slavs or Rumanians, as the case might
be, were in the majority, but also considerable
districts inhabited by Magyars. Some of these, as
parts of Transylvania, could not be left with Hungary without leaving a larger number of non-
Magyars in that country. Other districts lay right

on the frontiers, but were taken from Hungary, in spite of their populations, for economic or strategic reasons. In this way Rumania got, in round figures and according to the Hungarian census of 1910,[1] 1,700,000 Magyars, together with 2,800,000 Rumanians and 750,000 other nationalities; Czechoslovakia 1,050,000 Magyars, with 1,690,000 Slovaks, 420,000 Ruthenes and 325,000 others; and Yugoslavia (excluding Croatia, the cession of which Hungary recognized) 470,000 Magyars with 605,000 Serbs, Croats and other Yugoslavs, and 450,000 others.

THE POLICY OF REVISION. From the day on which the Hungarian delegates signed the Treaty of Trianon, the whole of Hungarian foreign policy could be summed up in the single word 'revision'—revision of the Treaty which had inflicted these losses on the Kingdom. Many Hungarians, of course, understood by 'revision' the complete restoration of 'historic Hungary'. They had been brought up in an intense pride in their ancient state, with its 'millenary frontiers' and in a firm belief that no other order was right, natural or even, in the long run, possible in the Danube basin. They had been taught to believe that the 'disloyalty' of the non-Magyars was simply the work of a few agitators, fomented from outside—from Rumania, Serbia or the anti-Hungarian forces in Austria. They believed that the peoples them-

[1] The census subsequently taken by all Successor States were, indeed, much less favourable to the Magyar element, but still showed large numbers of Magyars in each of these three States.

selves were attached to Hungary and readily accepted the rule in it of the Magyar or Magyarized oligarchy and that they had no real cause of complaint. Others admitted that the non-Magyars had had much to complain of, and had become disaffected, but put the blame solely on the unwise and intolerant policy of the governments of the past half century and thought that a different policy would have ensured the loyalty of the 'nationalists'.

This belief in the justification of historic Hungary and demand for 'integral revision' was most freely expressed by those Magyars whose homes had been in the non-Magyar districts now lost to Hungary. These included many Magyar landowners, whose estates had been situated among non-Magyar peasants, among whom they were divided up by the new governments. This gave the latter the excuse of representing the whole revisionist movement as the work of a few landowners anxious to save or to recover their estates. This was a misrepresentation: for the landowners, although they would have preferred to save their estates, would still have wished to remain in Hungary on any terms, and many other persons besides them believed in 'integral revision'. But it is true that the whole question was made more difficult by the widespread Hungarian belief that the whole structure of the Danube basin ought to be centralized in Budapest and run on a uniform system which could, under the circumstances, be only a Magyar national one; that only a State, Magyar in form, could deal with its problems. From this it was only a step to the attitude that the Magyars themselves were the natural superiors of their neighbours, a *Herrenvolk* acknowledging no equals except, indeed, the Germans.

This *Herrenvolk* attitude, which was so bitterly and so justly resented by Hungary's neighbours, represented, of course, the outlook of the ruling class, whose domination, in its social and political aspects, pressed just as heavily on the Magyar peasants and workers as on the non-Magyars. But it does not account for the whole of the Hungarian 'revisionism'. The poor man in Hungary cared nothing for the estates of the Transylvanian magnates, and did not challenge the right of the 'nationalities' to freedom. But even he felt the Treaty to be unjust, and agreed with his government at least in the wish for a 'lesser revision' which would restore to Hungary the Magyar populations now left just outside the frontiers.

THE REVISIONIST PURPOSE OF THE GERMAN ALLIANCE. Hungary ended by joining Germany again in the present war because Germany, like her a loser in the last war, also wished to upset the system which the victors had set up after it, and was thus the only power both willing and, perhaps, strong enough to help her to her 'revision'. Thus the Hungarian position and actions in the present war have been the direct outcome of the last. Indeed, the two are so closely interconnected that it is really hardly fair to speak of Hungary as following the same course 'twice in a generation'; the whole is really only one story.

Many Hungarians felt deep misgivings about the course which they ended by adopting. The pro-

German element was, indeed, constantly urging the closest possible friendship with Germany. They not only argued that no other country would help Hungary, but even if she could have chosen her helpers, they would have preferred Germany to be the choice, both as Hungary's 'natural ally' against the Slavs, and, after Hitler came into power, as the embodiment of counter-revolution, anti-Bolshevism and anti-Semitism. They ridiculed the idea that any force in the world would be able to stand up to the mighty German army.

Men who thought along these lines were very influential in Hungary, especially in the army, and were strongly represented in successive governments. General Gömbös, who was Hungarian Prime Minister in the early thirties, was one of them, and did much to lay the foundations of the later close co-operation between Hungary and Germany.

POSITION OF THE MODERATES. But not all Hungarians liked Hitler's ideas. There were, and are, many who hoped to see Hungary develop along more modern and more democratic lines. Then there was the old, widespread dislike of the Germans, inherited from the old revolts against the Austrian Emperors. There was a deep fear that if the Germans did win, their victory would not benefit the Hungarians, who would be enslaved just like all the other smaller peoples of Europe. Finally, a few of the more travelled and far-seeing Hungarian politicians knew something of the resources of the Western Powers and were not convinced that the German army was, after all, invincible.

The Hungarians who thought this way were still unwilling to ally themselves with the Little Entente, on the terms of giving up revision. But they looked for allies not to Germany, but to the two other nearby countries in something of the same position as themselves, Italy and Poland, and they always hoped that, if revision came, they could get the Western Powers to participate in arranging it or at any rate to approve it. The leader of this school of thought was Count Paul Teleki, who became Prime Minister for the second time in 1939 (he had held the same position for a short time in 1921).

MUNICH: ASCENDANCY OF THE PRO-GERMANS. No Hungarian Government, however, was prepared actually to refuse restoration of the Magyar areas if offered it, even by Germany, and things developed in a way which at first seemed to give the all-out-for-Germany party very much the best of the argument. Throughout the years after the war, when Germany was still weak, both Hungary's neighbours and the Western Powers supported the *status quo* in its entirety. In 1927 Hungary concluded a Treaty with Italy, and Mussolini publicly took up the Hungarian cause. But it soon appeared that Italy would never be able to give Hungary much more than words; and she moved over presently to the 'Axis'. Poland was even less of a help. Thus it appeared that after all, Hungary would never get anything unless Germany moved, and even then, she might not benefit unless she took care to be on good terms with Germany. In fact, when the first real chance came—at Munich in

1938—the Hungarian Government of the day nearly missed the boat altogether, for having been too independent toward Germany in the preceding months. Hurriedly they tried to make amends and ended by getting awarded to them the southern strip of Slovakia and Ruthenia at the expense of Czechoslovakia; but now they had to take it at the hands of Germany and Italy, with the Western Powers disapproving.

So things went on. The Hungarians occupied Ruthenia in March 1939, and represented what they did as a move against Germany; but in Britain it was regarded as another stab in the back of Czechoslovakia. Then came the invasion of Poland by Germany with Britain and France coming in to help Poland. At first the Hungarian Government tried to keep out, and were able to do so since Italy was following the same course. They even went so far as to bury their quarrel with Yugoslavia. But they were unwilling to do the same with Rumania, to whom Hungary had lost much more, both in area and population by the Treaty of Trianon. And Rumania had recently received a guarantee from Britain.

THE VIENNA AWARD. Thus when the chance of revision here came, in the summer of 1940—this time through Russia's action—Hungary again had to take it from the Axis, if at all. The result was the Second Vienna Award, of 30th August 1940, which gave Hungary Northern Transylvania.

The population in Transylvania is particularly mixed, and it is practically impossible to draw a line which does not favour one side or the other.

By this time the Rumanians had rejected the British guarantee of assistance to defend their independence and both Rumanians and Hungarians were competing for Germany's favour. The Hungarian Government got the better bargain of the two but at the price of further subservience to Germany. They had to sign the Three Power Pact, which allied them formally with the Axis. At the same time Teleki carried his policy of reconciliation with Yugoslavia further, and the two countries signed a Pact of Eternal Friendship. But this action, the first genuine renunciation of revisionist claims which any Hungarian Government had made since the Trianon, proved in the end the most fatal of all.

COUNT TELEKI'S SUICIDE AND ITS SIGNIFICANCE. For both Italy and Germany had now dropped the idea of keeping South-Eastern Europe out of the war. Italy had invaded Greece; Hitler was making his plans for attacking Russia and wanted the Balkans under his control. For this purpose he began sending troops into Rumania and Bulgaria. The Hungarian Government allowed these troops to pass through Hungary, and although this was a glaring breach of neutrality, the British Government did not call Hungary openly to account for it. But Hitler then made the same demand of Yugoslavia. The Yugoslav Government in Power— that with which Hungary had signed her Part of Friendship—agreed; but there was a revolt. A new Yugoslav Government came into Power, rejected the Germans' demands and prepared to fight, if necessary.

Hitler now prepared to invade Yugoslavia through Hungary, and called upon the Government in Budapest to give him facilities. Rewards were certainly promised for obedience, penalties for refusal. On 3 April 1941, when the German demands came before the Hungarian Government, the Prime Minister, Paul Teleki, although a devout Catholic, took his own life rather than commit so dishonourable an act; but the Regent did not follow his example and found a successor Bárdossy, to cover the shameful policy. Hungary not only let the German troops attack from her territory, but herself joined in the attack, being rewarded with part, although not all, of what she had lost to Yugoslavia through the Trianon Treaty (the Bačka, Baranya and two small areas in the west; the Yugoslav Banat was left to Serbia).

THE RUSSIAN 'CRUSADE'. In consequence of this, Britain broke off diplomatic relations with Hungary. Under Bárdossy's leadership, the Government was now completely subservient to Germany, and the final consequence of this was seen in June of the same year, when Hitler attacked Russia. Hungary had probably intended to remain neutral, but again pressure was brought to bear, again the Government's hand was forced, and again Bárdossy followed the suicidal policy to which he was committed, and Hungary embarked on the most fatal of all her adventures. In December, the British Empire and the U.S.A. declared war on Hungary. Although Hungary was now hopelessly committed to Germany and although the idea of a 'crusade against Bolshevism' had a certain appeal for the 'men of the counter-revolution' who still ruled the country, the war became unpopular enough as soon as it became clear that it was not to be a walk-over for the Germans and a trivial price for Hungary to pay for what she had previously received at Germany's hands. The German disaster at Stalingrad shook the Hungarians profoundly, and not long after it the forces which they themselves had reluctantly put in the field suffered a crushing defeat at Voronezh, where a great part of the Hungarian armies in the field and nearly all their heavy equipment were lost. A new Prime Minister, Kállay, tried painfully to find his way, at least part of the way, back. The bulk of the troops in Russia were recalled, the talk of a victorious crusade dropped. Towards Russia Hungary now protested that she was acting purely in self-defence and had not designs on a mile of territory; towards the Western Powers she claimed that she had no quarrel with them, and she tried by every means to convince them of the justice of her cause.

FALSE HOPES RAISED BY ITALIAN SURRENDER. If British and American troops had reached the frontiers of Hungary in 1943, the country would probably not have resisted, and a government might well have been found which would have turned, as Badoglio's Government in Italy turned, against Germany. It is no secret that the Left—the Socialists, Smallholders and others—to whom Kállay allowed a great deal of freedom, wished this course to be taken as soon as the debacle in Italy occurred. But the Western Allies remained fighting a difficult campaign in Southern Italy, and the half-hoped-for British landing in the Balkans did not occur. Soviet Russia was a different proposition in the eyes of the Government; and even Russia was still far from the frontiers of Hungary. The only Power on her doorstep was Germany. Meanwhile in the country the pro-German party redoubled its propaganda to show how terrible would be the results for Hungary of an Allied victory: Russo-Soviet influence over all Central Europe, Czech hegemony in it, a new and worse Trianon. Kállay could not make up his mind to do more than hesitate, and at last even his hesitation grew too much for the Germans. In March 1944, there was another crisis; more threats to the Regent, who yielded again. German troops marched into the country, Kállay took shelter in the Turkish Legation, a new and much more pro-German Government took office and once again, as after Teleki's suicide, the end of the period of double-dealing was proclaimed.

NAZI DOMINATION AND THE SHADOW OF DEFEAT. Of course, it was not the end. The new men had their way for a time. The leaders of the Left were interned, the Labour movement brought under new Fascist control, the Press disciplined. Above all, a violent persecution set in of the Jews, to whom the earlier governments, even Bárdossy's, had allowed a degree of freedom and protection unparalleled in German-controlled Europe. In a few short, dreadful weeks the Nazi's Hungarian henchmen inflicted fearful sufferings on the Jews, undoing all the good which their predecessors had done for Hungary by their relative decency. But soon, once again, as so many times before, Hungary was repenting at leisure what she had in haste committed, or allowed to be committed against her. Soon she was back in her old position of longing for a way out but not daring to take a decisive step.

The longer the Hungarians hesitated, the worse the position grew. Our declaration of war on Hungary had already placed that country in the position of an enemy versus a friend, as regards the frontiers with Czechoslovakia and Yugoslavia: Only with Rumania had the position been any better for Hungary, for although the British had not recognized the Vienna Award, Rumania had been an enemy to Britain equally with Hungary. But on 23 August 1944, Rumania at last accepted terms offered to her from Moscow some time previously, and these included recognition of the injustice of the Vienna Award. Now even Rumania was with the Allies; Hungary was left almost alone, surrounded by enemies and facing inevitable defeat.

CAUGHT IN THE TOILS. In this situation, the Regent's obstinate fear of Bolshevism at last yielded to the persuasion of more far-sighted advisers, and on 15 October 1944, Hungary was startled by a sudden, unheralded proclamation in which the Regent announced that he had asked the Allies for an armistice and had issued orders to the Army to cease hostilities. There was wild rejoicing among much of the war-weary people; but it was soon checked. The Germans, through their agents, had been precisely informed of what was afoot.

They occupied Budapest with German and pro-German Hungarian troops, seized the Regent and, after issuing in his name a recantation of his proclamation and a deed of abdication, carried him off to Germany in 'protective custody'. Under their armed patronage the 'Arrow Cross', a band of fanatical extremists, seized power. They were headed by an ex-officer of Armenian descent named Szálasi, who proclaimed himself 'Leader of the Nation' and issued the order to fight to the last. Although the Arrow Cross comprised only a small minority of the people, it was able, with German help, to suppress resistance in the capital and in West Hungary; the fight went on, while behind the line, the Germans hurriedly stripped the country bare. Corn, cattle, the contents of stores, warehouses and shops, machinery, even workers, where they could be induced to move, were hurriedly transported to Germany.

Meanwhile, the Russians advanced swiftly. Soon they were at the gates of Budapest and by Christmas had encircled it. A frightful battle now took place. The Germans, whose only care was to gain time for the construction of new defences in the Reich itself, defended Budapest street by street, house by house. They were helped by raw, fanatical levies of the Arrow Cross, some of the men desperate refugees, and a few factory workers, affected by the very Radical character of the Government's propaganda, and a few units of the Hungarian Army. Meanwhile, the wretched population, swollen by refugees to nearly 2,000,000, starving and deprived of light, heat and even water, lurked in cellars waiting for the end. When at last the capital was cleared of its defenders, what had been the pride of generations of Hungarians, was a mere smoking heap of ruins. Of all the capitals of the belligerents, on either side, not one, except only Warsaw, has suffered so dreadfully as Budapest.

THE PROVISIONAL GOVERNMENT. But the last act of this tragedy was not altogether without hope. Even while Budapest was undergoing its death-agony, news came from Debreczen—the historic city of Eastern Hungary in which Kossuth had proclaimed the separation of Hungary from Austria in 1849—that a new Provisional National Assembly, elected by local Resistance Councils and the liberated towns and villages, had met and had appointed a Provisional Government. The most prominent figures in it were high serving officers, two of whom had crossed over to the Russians in obedience to the Regent's proclamation of 15 October 1944, while the third had headed the armistice delegation to which the proclamation referred. The other members of the Government were drawn chiefly from the democratic and pro-Allied parties, which under the recent regime had been working underground, preparing for such a day as this. There were Smallholders, Social Democrats, Communists and some progressive non-Party men, including the son of Paul Teleki, who had committed suicide in 1941 in the hope of saving his country.[1]

[1] The reported composition of the Government, which certainly seemed representative enough, was as follows: *Prime Minister*, Gen. Bela Miklós de Dálnok (a Transylvanian Szekler not hitherto known in politics); *Under-*

The Government announced a programme of democratic and social reform, the restoration of the old liberties suppressed by the previous tyrannies, the repeal of anti-Jewish laws and the introduction of a radical land reform and of other urgent social measures.

At the same time, they accepted the consequences of defeat. War was declared on Germany. A new delegation went to Moscow and received from the Allies armistice terms which pledged Hungary to renunciation of whatever temporary gains of territory she had made at the expense of the United Nations, and to reparation for the losses which her policy had inflicted on them. A new army was to help Hungary to 'work her way home' by joining in the common fight against the remaining enemy.

CONCLUSION

The Provisional Hungarian Government promised to make a new start. It broke with Germany and with the policy of aggression. It promised to seek a peaceful and friendly relationship with the

Sec. of State, Rev. Istvan Balogh*; *Foreign Affairs*, János Gyöngyössy* (Smallholders' Party); *Interior*, Francis Erdei (National Peasants' Party); *Justice*, Agoston Valentini (Social Democrat); *Finance*, I. Vásaly (Smallholder); *War*, General János Vörös* (former Chief of Staff; commanded troops in Russia); *Supply*, Gen. Gabriel Faragó; *Industry*, Dr Takats (Social Democrat); *Trade*, Dr Joseph Gabór (Communist); *Social Services*, Dr Erik Molnár (Social Democrat); *Education*, Count Géza Teleki (Conservative); *Agriculture*, Imre Nagy (Communist).

* The three members of the second Armistice Delegation to Moscow.

U.S.S.R. and with the other United Nations, and with Hungary's neighbours. Its Premier, General Miklós, denounced the German influences which led Hungary into so many fatal adventures, and his colleagues promised social reforms which, if they could be carried through, would alter radically the whole structure of the country and make possible for it a new life. If the land of Hungary were fairly distributed among its people, so as to create a peasant class such as exists elsewhere in South-Eastern Europe; if the workers could become strong, free and independent; if political institutions could be made free and democratic, then it would no longer be possible to look on Hungary as a foreign body in Europe ruled by a caste whose mentality, social and political outlooks and ambitions disturbed the peace of South-Eastern Europe and proved a formidable obstacle to its solidarity.

The new Government was formed under Soviet auspices and welcomed by Moscow and in other quarters. But Hungary's troubles are, of course, not yet over. She has many very heavy trials ahead of her, both political and economic.

Right up to the summer of 1944, both the country and the people of Hungary had suffered, physically, less than most European states. The Hungarian Army had done comparatively little fighting and its losses had been correspondingly small. It had suffered one great disaster, at Voronezh, but after that Kállay had insisted on limiting further Hungarian military operations in Russia to the minimum. Budapest was hardly bombed before the spring of 1944, when the Allies made a series of attacks on the traffic points and military installations on the outskirts of the city.

Luxuries had, of course, soon become unobtainable for most of the people, but the supply of the necessities of life was fairly well maintained up to the summer of 1944. Clothes, other textiles and boots and shoes were in short supply but not absolutely lacking, and most of the essential foods were available in sufficient, although not luxurious, quantities.

But this position was only made possible by drawing dangerously on reserves and mortgaging the future. The fields were exhausted by overcropping and under-manuring. The animal population had dwindled dangerously. The scanty stock of agricultural machinery, and even of ordinary implements and tools, had begun to run low and could not be replenished. Moreover, labour shortage on the land had become acute, in consequence of mobilization.

In the factories, much machinery was turned over to war production. This would need to be reconverted for peace production. There was little replacement of worn-out machinery for a full five years. The transport system was also getting worn out. There was a general and growing housing shortage.

But all this would still have left Hungary in a position which most Continental countries could have envied if the war had not reached her in the autumn of 1944. When it did come, it came very severely. The Soviet armies were able to sweep through Rumania. In most parts of Yugoslavia the fighting was on the guerilla scale, except along the main lines of communication. In Bulgaria there was practically no fighting at all. But in Hungary the Soviet armies had to fight for every yard of their advance, and so places where the Germans made their chief stands, above all Budapest, experienced all the horrors and destruction of the front line. To this must be added the wholesale spoliation of the country carried through in their retreat by the Germans and by that party of Hungarians who chose to evacuate Hungary with the retreating Germans, taking with them everything on which they could lay hands. Finally, the systematic destruction by the retreating armies of railways, bridges and other means of communications put the crowning touch on the economic ruin.

Another problem likely to prove a very acute one is that of refugees. When the Soviet armies began their advance across Hungary very many Hungarians fled before them, out of fear either of the Soviets, or simply of becoming involved in the fighting. They crowded into west Hungary, which they believed would be safe, and were overtaken there by the new Soviet advance. Some of these refugees will have returned to their homes once the fighting passed over them, but the end of the war, like the end of the last war, will bring a long-term refugee problem arising out of the return to narrower frontiers. Officials and their families, colonists and other persons who had made their homes in areas awarded to Hungary by the Axis, or seized in 1941, will need to make a fresh start inside the new frontiers. If it is decided to make an exchange of any minorities, e.g. with

Rumanians, the number of persons needing resettlement in Hungary will be very greatly increased.

Even the reforms promised by the Provisional Government will need money, if they are to be real. There cannot be a solid working class unless it finds employment in the factories. Land reform, by general consent the most important measure of all, is not a cheap process. Leaving entirely aside the question of compensation for expropriated owners, the new peasant proprietors will need implements, stocks, seeds and credits. In many cases it will be necessary to build new houses and sometimes whole villages, with communications and services; for otherwise the land available for allocation would be useless to the recipients, as lying too far from their homes. Among the middle classes there is the devastation caused by the horrible destruction of the Jewish communities to be repaired.

The new Hungarian democracy thus starts its career under a heavy handicap. And it will certainly not be free from political difficulties inside the country itself. The loss of any war breeds bitterness, and the bitterness in Hungary, whose partnership with Germany brought her such substantial temporary gains taken from her once more by the United Nations, is likely to be considerable. There will be dissension and unhappiness, and the greater the severity of the settlement meted out to Hungary, the harder will it be for the new leaders to show that their course is the best in the interests of all.

The responsibilities, as well as the opportunities,

if the Allies as a whole make the final settlement,
will be great. It is true, as these pages have shown,
that the old Hungary was characterized by much
that had long outlived what usefulness it ever possessed: much social injustice, much political reaction, as well as the maintenance of many claims
against Hungary's neighbours, arising out of past
history, which the new world has decided to regard
as finally unacceptable. It is also true that in international affairs the old rule still prevails that the
loser pays. Neither Hungary nor any other country
which gambled on a German victory can hope to
escape the loss of its stake when Germany is
defeated.

Nevertheless, the political structure of South-
Eastern Europe can hardly be secure if Hungary's
position in it is of a sort which even democratic
and progressive Hungarians reject in their hearts,
nor can the economic rehabilitation of the same
area be complete without an orderly and prosperous
Hungary. And in Hungary and in the Hungarian
people—who have had little voice in the disastrous
decisions of their masters—there are many sterling
qualities for which the world can well find a use.
Europe will be the poorer and European peace the
less solid if it fails to do so.

INDEX

Printed in the United States
By Bookmasters